Cars

A COMPLETE HISTORY

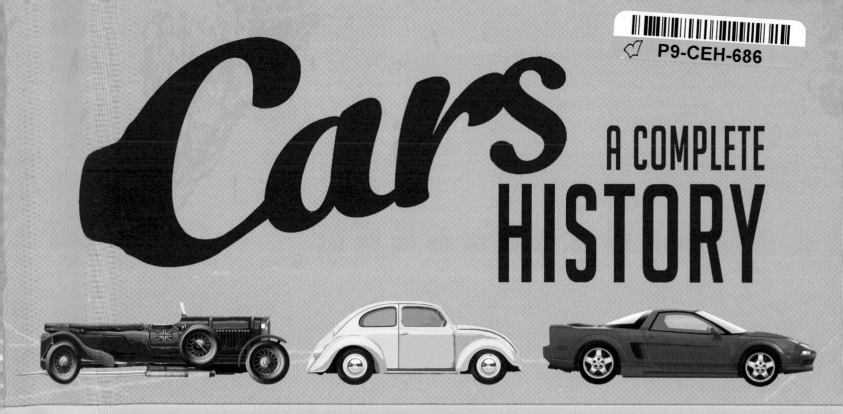

CONTENTS

Thunder Bay Press
An imprint of Printers Row Publishing Group
10350 Barnes Canyon Road, Suite 100, San Diego, CA 92121
www.thunderbaybooks.com

Printers Row Publishing Group is a division of Readerlink Distribution Services, LLC. Thunder Bay Press is a registered trademark of Readerlink Distribution Services, LLC.
All notations of errors or omissions should be addressed to Thunder Bay Press, Editorial Department, at the above address. All other correspondence (author inquiries, permissions)
concerning the content of this book should be addressed to Quarto Publishing, The Old Brewery, 6 Blundell Street, London, N7 9BH, UK

ISBN: 978-1-62686-154-1

Made in Shenzhen, China
22 21 20 19 18 6 7 8 9 10

Paper engineers Richard Ferguson, Alan Brown; **Designers** Alan Brown, Simon Morse; **Illustrators** Mat Edwards, Jerry Pyke, Nigel Chilvers, Stefano Azzalin
Managing Editor Diane Pengelly; **Creative Director** Jonathan Gilbert; **Publisher** Zeta Jones

HOW TO BUILD YOUR MODELS

BASIC TECHNIQUES

Specific instructions for building
each model are detailed from
page 103 onward.
   Basic techniques that are
used in many of the models are
illustrated here.

SHAPING Before assembling the
model, fold the main bodywork
into shape along the creased
lines, using the photograph of the
finished model as a guide.

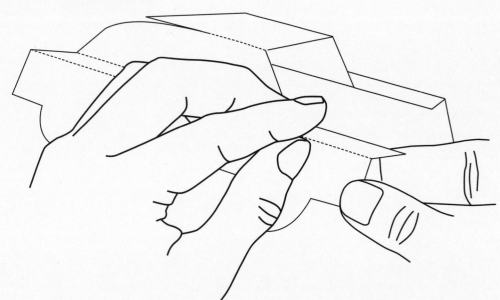

ROUNDING Where rounded
pieces are required, use a
round pencil to help shape
the card. Wind the piece
carefully around the pencil,
keeping the tension even as
you turn, and then release.

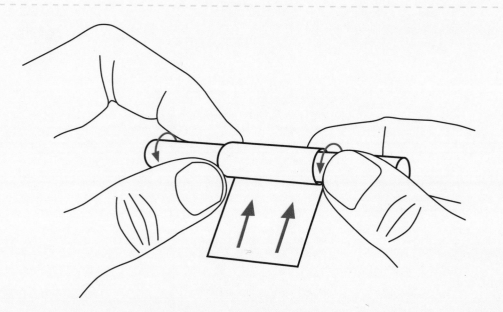

INTRODUCTION

Henry Ford was working hard every night, trying to build his first prototype car in his wooden shed. Neighbors called him "Crazy Henry." The ambitious young engineer had the last laugh, though: at two o'clock in the morning in June 1896, he burst through the shed wall at the wheel of a fully working car, and careered off on a gleeful tour of Detroit.

Even this great American auto pioneer, however, couldn't have foreseen how early 19th-century prototypes like his would develop into something so popular, so sophisticated, and so important over the course of the next century. In his own lifetime Henry went from constructing that original machine to building more than 15 million Model T cars. And that was just one model from the tens of thousands of different types that have been built since then. Cars certainly seem to have been a success story: there are an estimated 800 million of them on the world's roads today.

Our cities, our work, and our very lives have become organized around that strange new machine that Henry drove through his shed wall. Cars are now a major part of modern life. They may have become controversial in the debate about the world's environment, and increasingly manufacturers are obliged to reduce the pollution they cause, but cars are still one of the most desired material objects on the planet.

1

1

2

SECURED TABS Some elements are secured using tabs with "locking triangles," or lugs. These tabs are always inserted into a slot with a corresponding number.

1. Fold the lugs inward so that the tab becomes the same width as the corresponding slot.
2. Push the tab, lugs folded, into the slot.
3. Open out the lugs. The tab is now secured inside the slot.

3

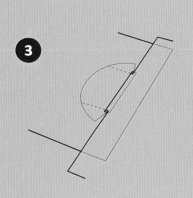

WHEELS When sticking a wheel to an axle, line up the fold of the tab with the center line of the wheel. Make sure that the tab is centered horizontally as well as vertically.

We drive cars for fun, to work, to shop, to get married, to the hospital to give birth, and we're even driven to the graveyard at the end of our lives. So perhaps it's not a surprise that some of us spend so much time thinking about them. If any readers are lucky enough to win the lottery, it's pretty certain that one of the first items on their shopping lists will be a car they've always dreamed of.

That makes writing a book like this a very tricky job. Which cars should be included? Everyone's idea of the most important 50 is different, and even the greatest auto experts will disagree on which are the most crucial cars of all time.

We've tried to select the best possible 50 by choosing a cross section of some of the most important, lovable, and downright interesting cars throughout history. It was a long, hard process and the resulting list should include at least some that every reader can agree deserve a place.

We can certainly be confident that these 50 cars demonstrate the complete history of the automobile, as well as a fair bit about our own social and cultural history. You'll be able to see how cars develop from Henry Ford's original mass-produced car, the Model T, to the latest super luxury car, the Rolls-Royce Wraith. Another thing we can say for certain: there isn't a boring car among them.

No one in the world owns all 50 of these iconic machines. And it's hard to imagine that anyone has even managed to drive them all. But with this book, all car lovers can enjoy reading about them, dreaming about them and, thanks to some brilliant designers and paper engineers, making great models of every single one.

BASIC TECHNIQUES

CURVES Some card elements have triangular tabs with a score line at their base. These are not sticking tabs; they are designed to help support the shape of the model.

Fold them to sit at the same angle as the sticking tabs, but do not glue them into place.

1908 FORD MODEL T

Henry Ford used new mass-production techniques to create the first car that almost everyone could afford. The Model T wasn't innovative, fast, or luxurious, but it was cheap—and it had the first fitted car radio. It was so successful that by 1918 half the cars in America were Model Ts. Almost 17 million were made in its 19-year production run.

Luxuries arrived slowly. By 1915 Model Ts had doors, a roof, and lights.

3

1908 FORD MODEL T

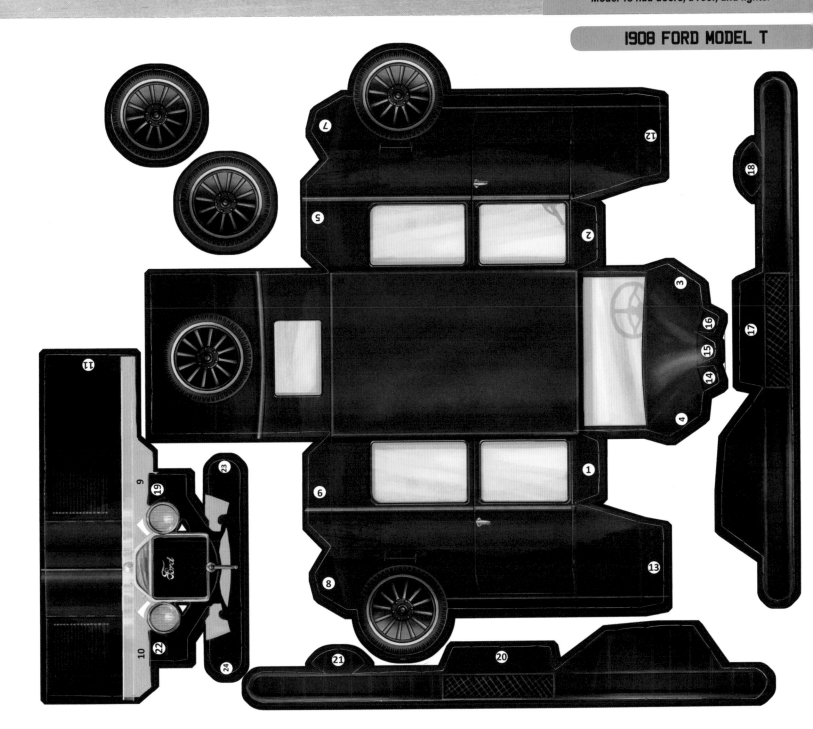

FEATURES:

- *Engine size* 177 cu. in.
- *Top speed* 45 mph
- *Acceleration 0–60 mph* Unknown
- *Power* 20 hp

FORD MODEL T

Ford's famous slogan for the Model T, "You can have any color as long as it's black," summed up the appeal of this no-frills car. In fact, black didn't become compulsory until 1914. That was when Ford discovered black was the quickest-drying paint, which sped up production and further reduced costs.

Drivers changed gear using three specially marked pedals.

4

1910 CADILLAC MODEL 30

Before the Model 30, many cars didn't have a roof, side doors, and windows—or even a windshield. Driving in bad weather was very uncomfortable, and even in good conditions mud and stones would be thrown up into the cabin. The 30 started Cadillac's reputation for luxury by fully enclosing the cabin for the first time.

Wooden artillery wheels added a touch of class.

5

1910 CADILLAC MODEL 30

FEATURES:

- *Engine size* 255 cu. in.
- *Top speed* 60 mph
- *Acceleration 0–60 mph* Unknown
- *Power* 32 hp

CADILLAC MODEL 30

Cadillac founder Henry Leland had built the first enclosed cabin for his personal one-cylinder car as early as 1905. Unfortunately, this was so top-heavy it often tipped over—with Leland still inside. The Model 30 of 1910 was better balanced, and within a decade almost all cars were available with a fully weatherproof cabin.

The Cadillac 30 pioneered the electric starter to replace hand cranking.

6

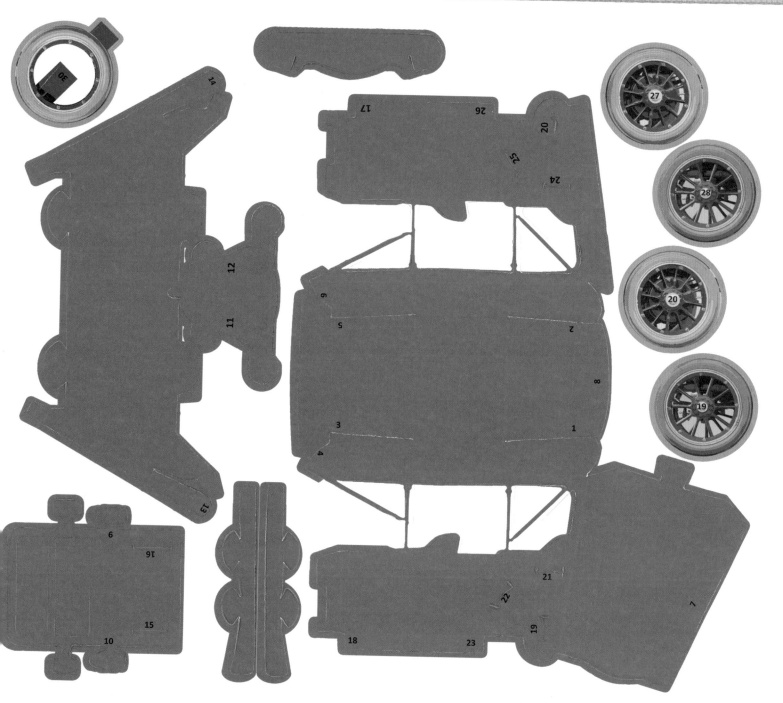

1928 DUESENBERG MODEL J

The Duesenberg brothers set out to design "the greatest car in the world." Many thought they succeeded. The Model J was revealed to huge acclaim at the 1928 New York Car Show and this fast, powerful automobile became the most fashionable car to own. It attracted glamorous buyers such as Greta Garbo and Al Capone.

The Model J was a favorite of gangsters and bootleggers.

7

1928 DUESENBERG MODEL J

FEATURES:

- *Engine size* 420 cu. in.
- *Top speed* 116 mph
- *Acceleration 0–60 mph* 13 seconds
- *Power* 265 hp

DUESENBERG MODEL J

The platforms along the side of the Model J that linked the two wheel-arches were called running boards. They were a common feature in cars of the era and usually used as a step for passengers to climb aboard. Gangsters' henchmen used them in a more sinister way, riding along on the outside of the boss's car wielding their guns.

The Model J was America's fastest road car.

8

1929 BENTLEY BLOWER

The idea was to boost the power of this huge, heavy car by adding a supercharger, or "blower." The car was over 14 feet long and weighed a hefty 4,250 pounds. The engine had only four cylinders but, thanks to the blower, was capable of well over 100 mph, making it one of the supercars of the late 1920s.

Bentley's supercharger was clearly visible in front of the hood.

1929 BENTLEY BLOWER

FEATURES:

- *Engine size* 268 cu. in.
- *Top speed* 130 mph
- *Acceleration 0–60 mph* 8 seconds
- *Power* 242 hp

Classic Bentley: leather, wood, and lots of dials.

BENTLEY BLOWER
The supercharger was like an early version of today's turbo. It was an air compressor, driven mechanically by the engine, that pumped extra air into the cylinders to boost power. Conservative owner Walter Owen Bentley, known simply as "W. O.," didn't approve of this "corruption," so superchargers were mounted outside the engine bay and could clearly be seen at the front of the car.

1930 PACKARD EIGHT

The huge Packard Eight outsold Cadillac and Lincoln and became the most prestigious American car. This eight-cylinder model was 12 feet between the wheels and weighed more than 5,000 pounds. Buyers were seduced by sophisticated engineering such as front-wheel brakes, four-speed gears, hydraulic shock absorbers, and a self-lubrication system.

Many Packards were traditionally hand-built by skilled workers.

11

1930 PACKARD EIGHT

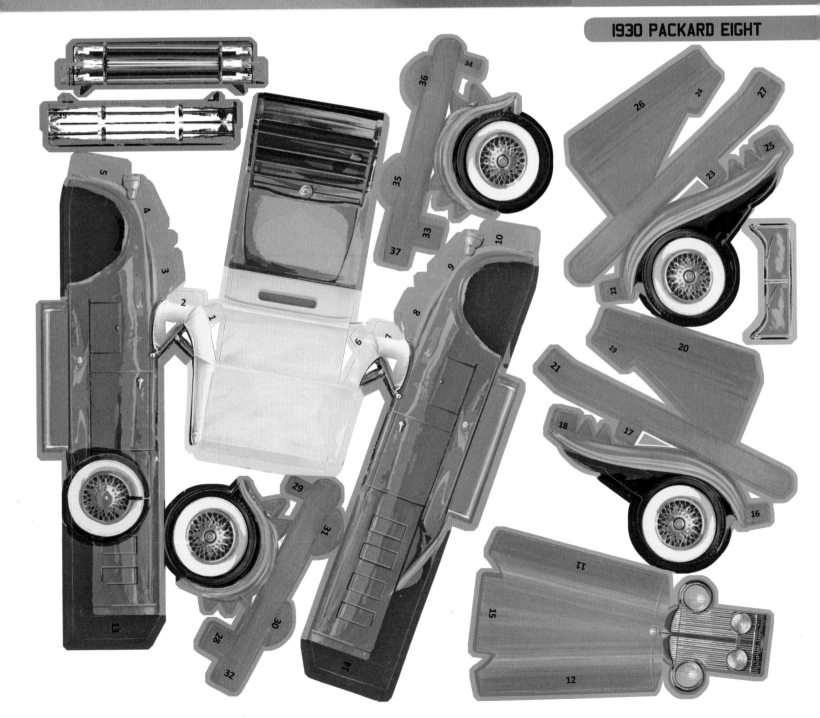

FEATURES:

- *Engine size* 385 cu. in.
- *Top speed* 85 mph
- *Acceleration 0–60 mph* 17 seconds
- *Power* 106 hp

PACKARD EIGHT

The Packard's interior was as luxurious as cars could be in 1930. The upholstery was high-quality leather, the dashboard a single piece of polished wood, and the floors covered with thick carpet. The front seats were usually arranged as one long bench, and the rear seat looked like a plush modern sofa.

Packard interiors were beautifully crafted.

12

1932 FORD MODEL B

The Model B took over when the Model T's sales began to falter. It was still modestly priced (from $495) but it was lower, sleeker, and faster than the T. Ford used all his production skills to make the B available in a variety of styles: as a roadster, saloon, station wagon, van, pickup, and coupé.

The humble Ford soon became the hot-rodders' favorite.

13

1932 FORD MODEL B

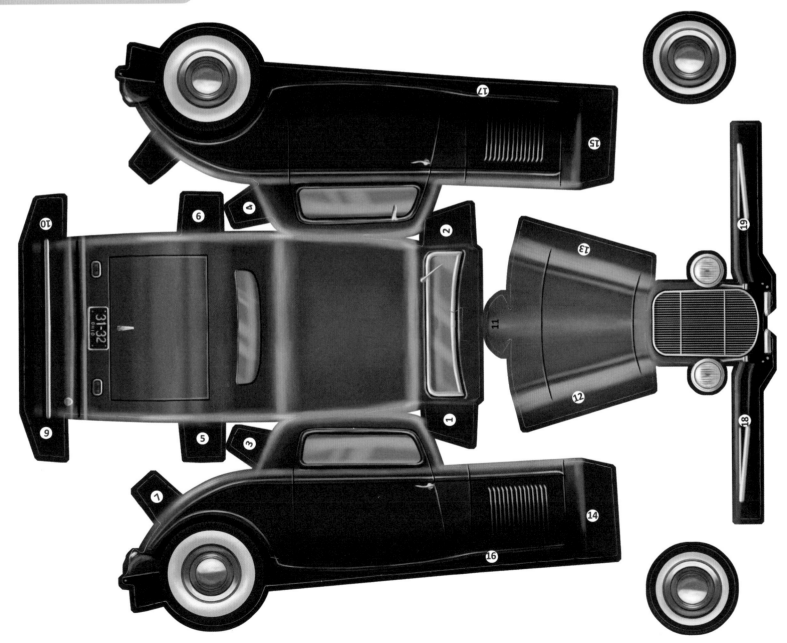

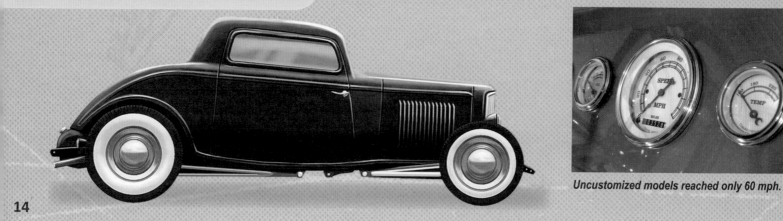

FEATURES:

- *Engine size* 124 cu. in.
- *Top speed* 65 mph
- *Acceleration 0–60 mph* Unknown
- *Power* 106 hp

FORD MODEL B

The sheet-metal body and four-cylinder engine were easy to customize, so the B became the world's first hot rod. After the war, virtually every available Model B was modified. The 1932 coupés were particularly prized and became known as the "Deuce Coupé." The Beach Boys' 1963 album *Little Deuce Coupe* was named in their honor.

Uncustomized models reached only 60 mph.

14

1933 AUTO UNION TYPE C

Auto Union racing cars dominated the tracks before World War II, thanks to their sophisticated engineering. The Type C "Silver Arrow" featured a rear supercharged V16 engine, streamlined aluminum body, and all-around independent suspension. Technical expertise came from Ferdinand Porsche and funding from the Nazis, who realized that motoring success would boost propaganda.

Most drivers struggled to control the Silver Arrow's high power and uneven weight distribution.

1933 AUTO UNION TYPE C

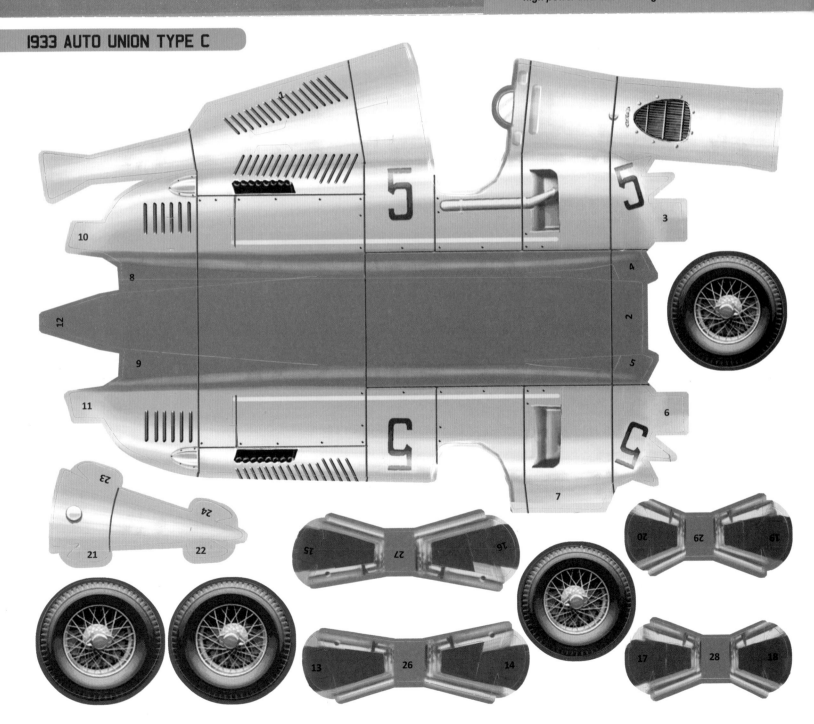

FEATURES:

- *Engine size* 366 cu. in.
- *Top speed* 236 mph
- *Acceleration 0–60 mph* Unknown
- *Power* 520 hp

AUTO UNION TYPE C

Overzealous acceleration could produce wheel-spin at speeds up to 150 mph. The extraordinary top speed was achieved by only a handful of drivers on the longest straight sections of track, but was decades ahead of its time.

Huge steering wheels were typical of the era.

16

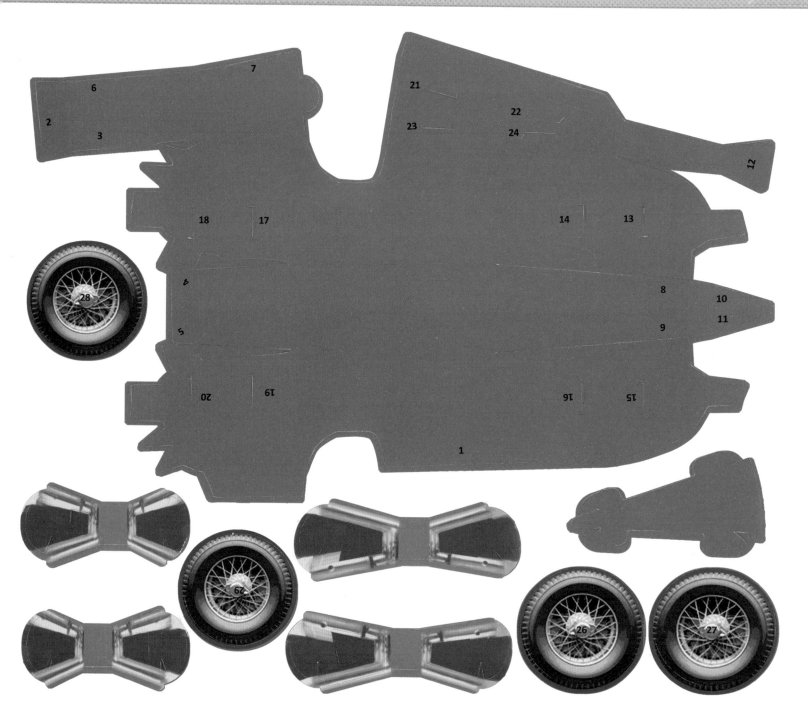

1934 CHRYSLER AIRFLOW

Engineers were reputedly inspired by the airships of their day to produce the first aerodynamic car. Months of pioneering testing in a wind tunnel convinced Chrysler that contemporary auto design was causing too much drag, increasing fuel consumption and slowing down cars. The result was revolutionary: boxy shapes were replaced with curves and the lights and grille were built flush with the body.

Chrysler engineers experimented to find the perfect aerodynamic car shape.

17

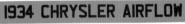

1934 CHRYSLER AIRFLOW

FEATURES:

- *Engine size* 323 cu. in.
- *Top speed* 95 mph
- *Acceleration 0–60 mph* 19.5 seconds
- *Power* 130 hp

CHRYSLER AIRFLOW

The Airflow design was way ahead of its time—and Chrysler's slogan was: "The first real motorcar." Sadly, it looked so futuristic that customers didn't like it. Sales were poor and within four years Chrysler stopped building it, but its aerodynamic features were eventually incorporated into mainstream car design.

Even the spare-wheel cover was aerodynamic.

18

1937 BUGATTI TYPE 57 ATLANTIC

Often called the world's most beautiful car, the Type 57 Atlantic is also one of the rarest and most valuable. Bugatti made around 700 Type 57s but only four had the curvaceous Atlantic shape. Only two survive. Millionaire fashion designer Ralph Lauren owns one; the other was bought by a California museum for $30 million in 2010.

The Atlantic's body was made of aluminum rather than steel.

19

1937 BUGATTI TYPE 57 ATLANTIC

FEATURES:

- *Engine size* 198 cu. in.
- *Top speed* 120 mph
- *Acceleration 0–60 mph* 10 seconds
- *Power* 200 hp

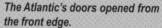

The Atlantic's doors opened from the front edge.

BUGATTI TYPE 57

The Bugatti was one of the most glamorous cars on the road but it also won the Le Mans 24-hour race in 1937 and 1939. The Type 57 was designed by founder Ettore Bugatti's son Jean. Tragically, when 30-year-old Jean tried the 1939 Le Mans winning car for himself near the Bugatti factory in Molsheim, he crashed and died.

1939 VOLKSWAGEN BEETLE

Hitler ordered German carmaker Ferdinand Porsche to design a "people's car" that could carry a family of five and cost under 1,000 Reichmarks. At the time, that was little more than the cost of a motorcycle. Porsche's Beetle was so successful that it went on to sell more than 21 million models, making it one of the most popular cars of all time.

Beetle production continued until 2003.

1939 VOLKSWAGEN BEETLE

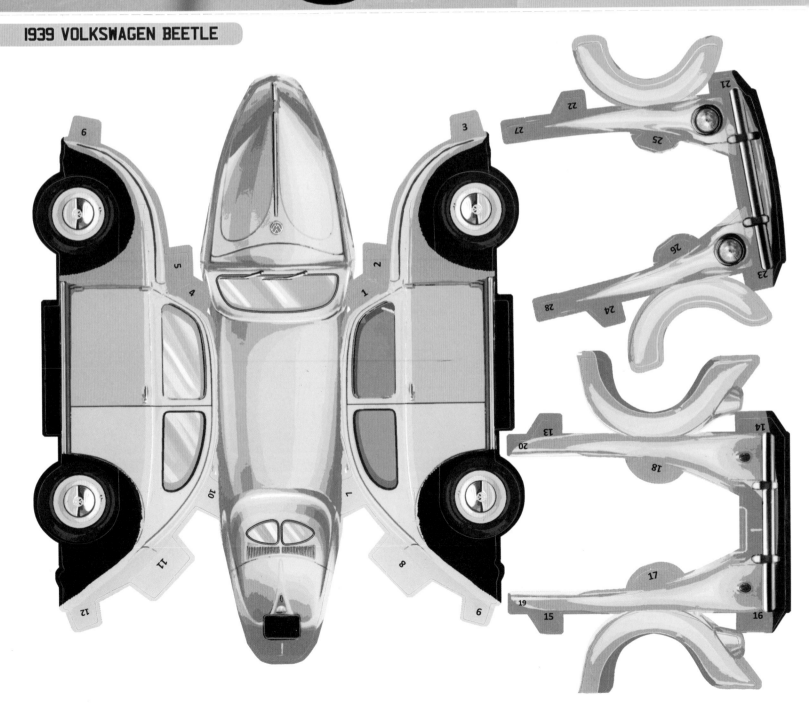

FEATURES:

- *Engine size* 60 cu. in.
- *Top speed* 56 mph
- *Acceleration 0–60 mph* Unknown
- *Power* 29 hp

*Porsche's trademark:
the engine in the back.*

VOLKSWAGEN BEETLE

Porsche's design used a small rear-mounted flat-four engine and a simple aerodynamic body shape. The big round headlamps and curved hood gave the Volkswagen a cheery character that remained fashionable right through the 1960s. As "Herbie," the Beetle even became the star of a series of Disney films.

22

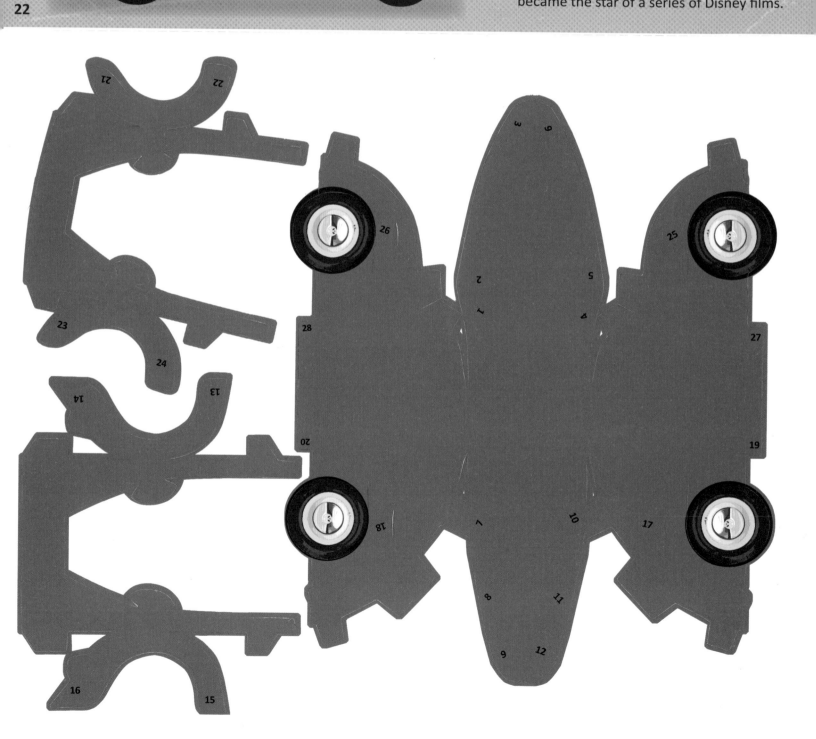

1941 WILLYS JEEP

The world's first mass-produced off-roader was crucial to the Allies' victory in World War II. At the request of the U.S. government, the military utility vehicle was hastily designed in 49 days. It was immediately built in huge numbers and its name became a generic term for what is now called an SUV or four-by-four.

The simple, rugged Jeep could pull 25 tons.

23

1941 WILLYS JEEP

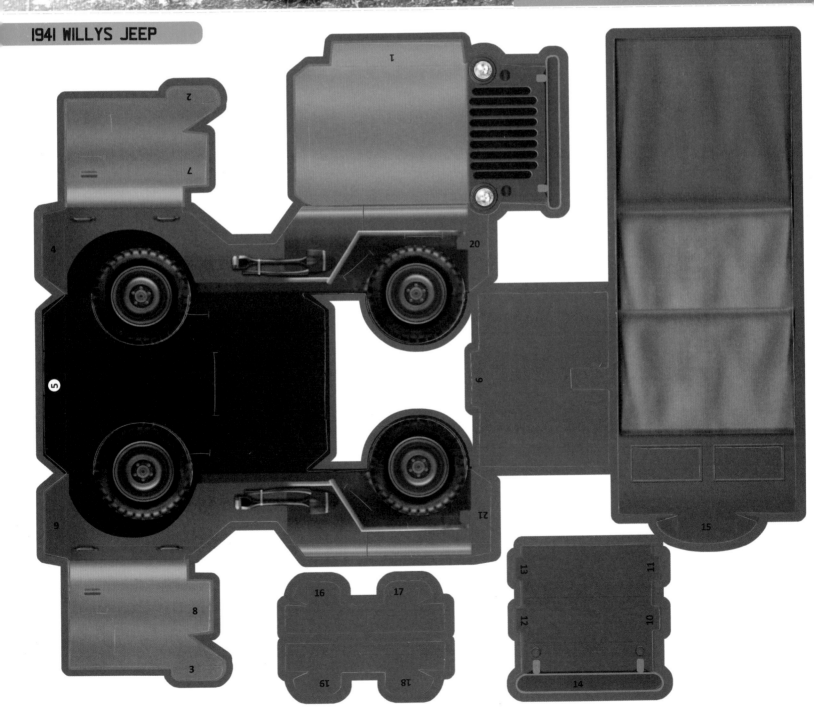

FEATURES:

- *Engine size* 134 cu. in.
- *Top speed* 60 mph
- *Acceleration 0–60 mph* Unknown
- *Power* 60 hp

The Jeep could climb slopes up to 40 degrees in all conditions.

WILLYS JEEP

The Jeep used a pioneering four-wheel-drive system that sent power to all four wheels rather than to just two, as had been the case in every production car until then. This allowed it to tackle a wide range of difficult terrain.

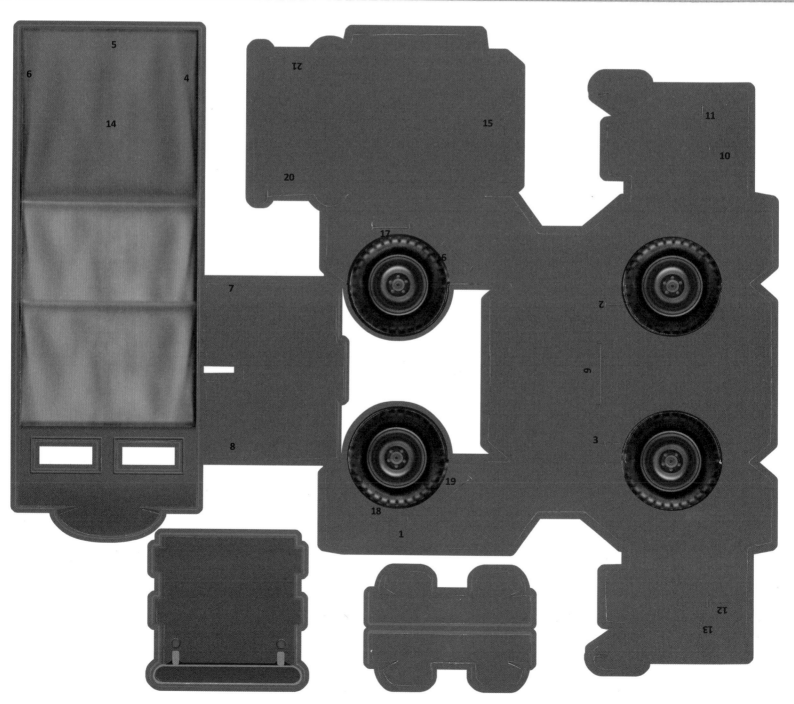

1948 CITROËN 2CV

Like a Gallic version of the Volkswagen, the 2CV was planned as a budget car for the predominantly rural population of France. The designer's brief was simple: it had to be able to carry four people plus 110 pounds of farm goods at 30 mph. The 2CV might even have predated the Beetle, had the war not delayed its launch.

The 2CV is known as the "deux chevaux"— "two horses" in French.

1948 CITROËN 2CV

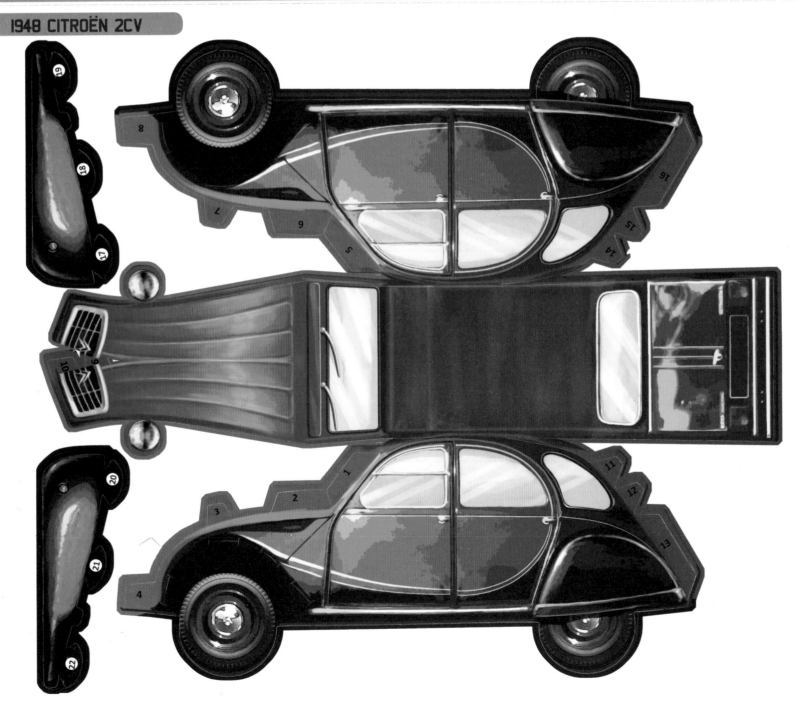

FEATURES:

- *Engine size* 22 cu. in.
- *Top speed* 40 mph
- *Acceleration 0–60 mph* Unknown
- *Power* 9 hp

CITROËN 2CV

The 2CV was designed to be ultra-simple and practical for country-dwellers. The high ground clearance and long-travel suspension helped it drive across the roughest tracks, and the roll-back fabric roof wasn't just for sunny days: when the trunk lid was unscrewed and the roof removed, the car turned into a mini pickup truck.

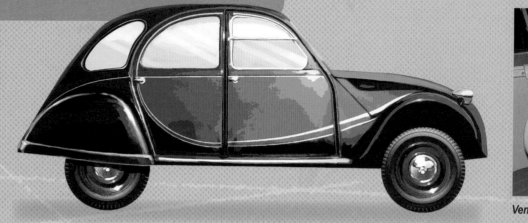

Ventilation was simply a hole in the dashboard.

1954 CADILLAC FLEETWOOD 60

Many Americans dreamed of owning a huge chrome-coated Cadillac in the fifties. Young rock-and-roll star Elvis Presley bought a blue Caddy and had it sprayed pink for his mother, Gladys. But she had no license, so Elvis and his band used the car to drive to concerts.

Elvis's Cadillac is still displayed at his old home at Graceland.

27

1954 CADILLAC FLEETWOOD 60

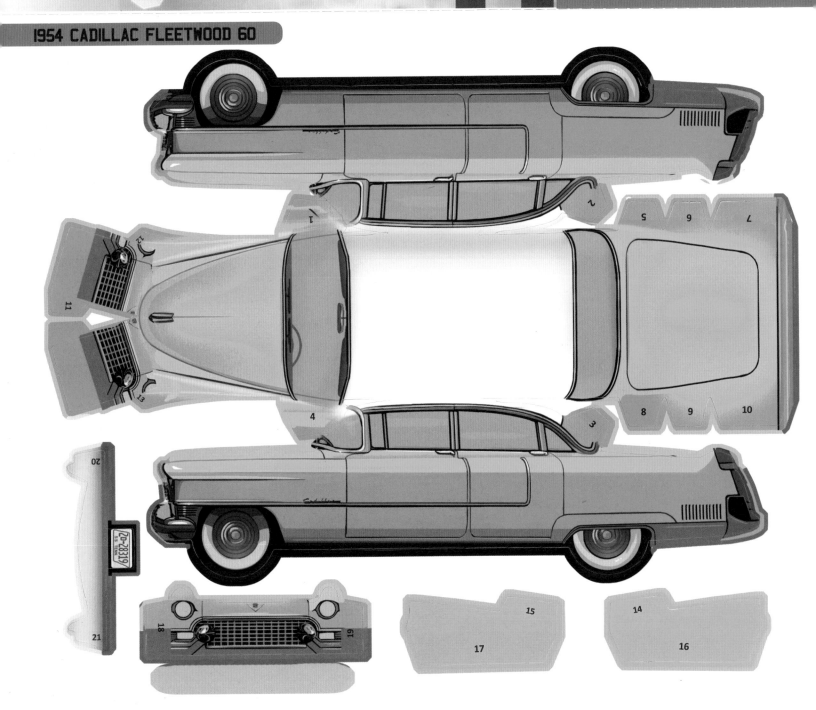

FEATURES:

- *Engine size* 331 cu. in.
- *Top speed* 104 mph
- *Acceleration 0–60 mph* 14.2 seconds
- *Power* 270 hp

CADILLAC FLEETWOOD 60

The 1954 "Super Sixty" was a typical gas-guzzling symbol of American carefree affluence. It was almost 19 feet long, weighed a hefty 4,670 pounds, and the thirsty 5.4-liter V8 engine with its four-speed automatic gearbox drank gas at around 12 mpg. In 1955 the Fleetwood cost around $4,700.

A heater and radio cost extra.

28

1955 CITROËN DS

When the "space age" DS was unveiled at the 1955 Paris Motor Show, suddenly every other car looked old-fashioned. On that first day alone, Citroën sold 12,000 models. From the groundbreaking use of aluminum and fiberglass to the first powered disk brakes and semi-automatic gearbox, the DS was way ahead of its time.

Styled by Italian sculptor Flaminio Bertoni, the DS was admired for its futuristic design.

29

1955 CITROËN DS

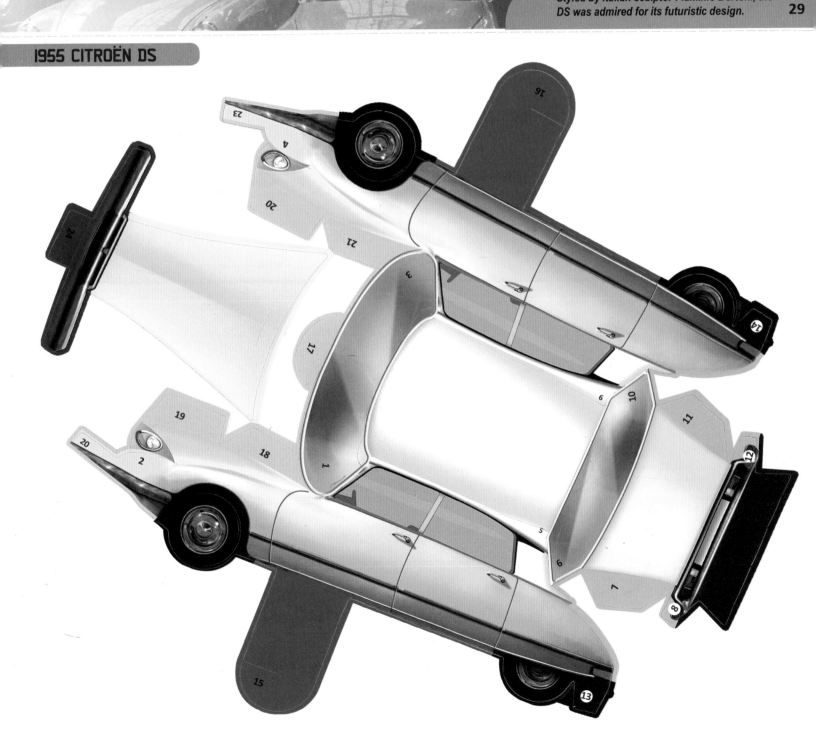

FEATURES:

- *Engine size* 117 cu. in.
- *Top speed* 87 mph
- *Acceleration 0–60 mph* 23 seconds
- *Power* 75 hp

The steering wheel had just one spoke.

CITROËN DS

The Citroën's self-leveling gas suspension dispensed with springs but kept the car at a constant height above the road. It could even be driven on three wheels, as President de Gaulle happily discovered when a would-be assassin's bomb blew a wheel off the car he was traveling in. Innovation continued inside with the first plastic dashboard and a single-spoke steering wheel, which safely collapsed on impact.

1956 CHECKER MOTOR CORPORATION A8

The Marathon was used as the taxi for New York and other U.S. cities. It was robust, reliable, and had a spacious back seat and an enormous trunk. Checker boasted that these were 200,000-mile cars and the model was put on normal sale. But the simple durable features appealed less to the public, and the vast majority were bought and used as taxis.

The Checker's starring roles in films and television shows ranged from Taxi Driver to Friends.

31

1956 CHECKER MOTOR CORPORATION A8

FEATURES:

- *Engine size* 226 cu. in.
- *Top speed* 93 mph
- *Acceleration 0–60 mph* 14 seconds
- *Power* 80 hp

CHECKER MOTOR CORPORATION A8

The Marathon's utilitarian details met the demands of life as a hardworking taxi. It had rubber mats rather than carpets, flat floors, hardboard ceilings, and replaceable bolt-on body panels.

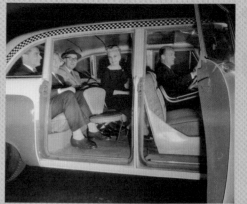

The A8 remains the most famous taxi in the United States.

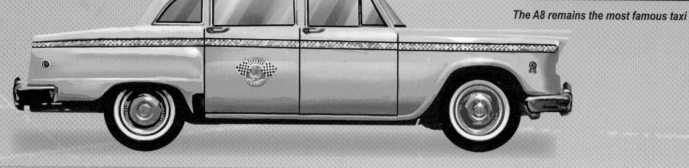

1957 VEB TRABANT

This primitive little vehicle was a symbol of life behind the Iron Curtain during the Cold War. It was unheard of in the West but, when the Berlin Wall was demolished, thousands of East Germans appeared at the wheel of these strange cars. From 1957 to 1991, a factory in Zwickau churned out three million of them.

The Trabant became a symbol of life behind the Iron Curtain.

1957 VEB TRABANT

FEATURES:

- *Engine size* 37 cu. in.
- *Top speed* 70 mph
- *Acceleration 0–60 mph* 21 seconds
- *Power* 26 hp

A Trabant was painted on the Berlin Wall as if crashing through it.

VEB TRABANT

The Trabant had a steel frame with plastic resin body panels bolted on. The tiny two-stroke, two-cylinder engine was more like a motorcycle engine but could be easily maintained by owners. Drivers had to add oil every time they filled with gas and there was no fuel gauge. Instead, you had to use a dipstick in the gas tank.

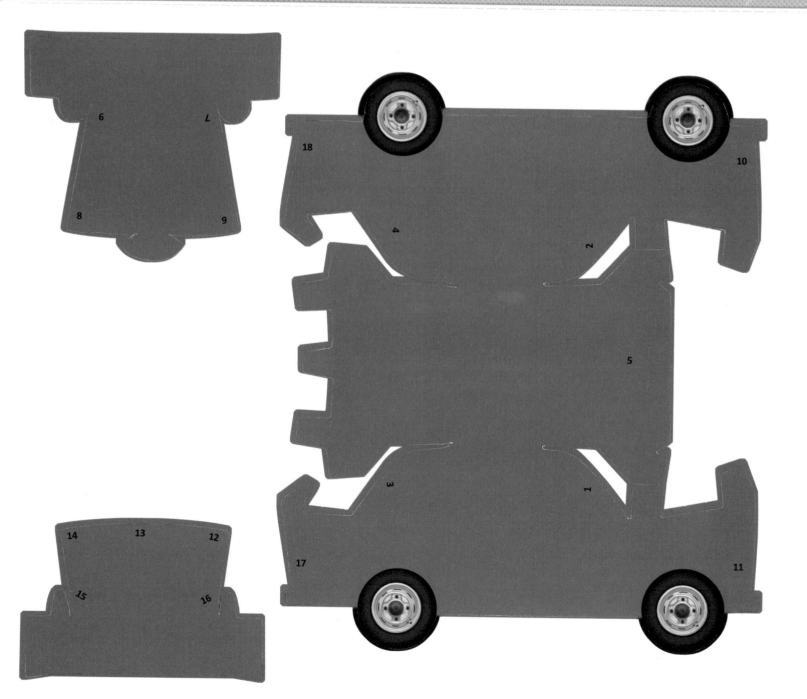

1959 ALFA ROMEO GIULIETTA SPIDER

Alfa's open-top cars were all "Spiders." They included the iconic 1960s car driven by Dustin Hoffman in *The Graduate*, and the hot 2006 incarnation, powered by a 146-mph V6 engine.

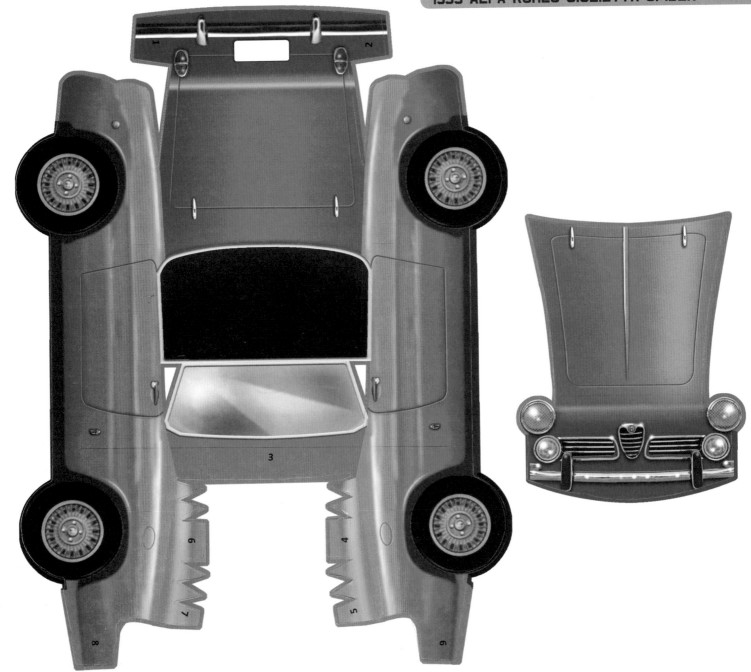

Progress in the Giulietta was spirited rather than fast, but this car was all about enjoyment.

35

1959 ALFA ROMEO GIULIETTA SPIDER

FEATURES:

- *Engine size* 79 cu. in.
- *Top speed* 100 mph
- *Acceleration 0–60 mph* 12.3 seconds
- *Power* 62 hp

The Alfa had a no-frills appeal.

ALFA ROMEO GIULIETTA SPIDER
The Giulietta's technical appeal was simple: there was a simple four-speed manual gearbox, and crisp handling thanks to the lightweight body, well-tuned suspension, unassisted direct steering, and rear-wheel-drive system. The small four-cylinder engine had a sophisticated twin-overhead cam arrangement that gave it an attractive rasping sound and responsiveness, especially at high revs.

36

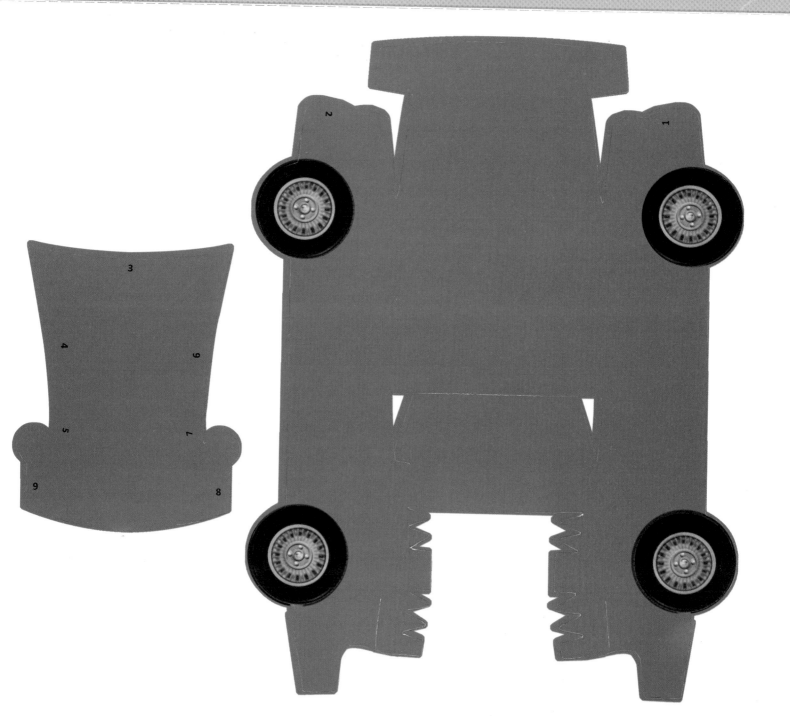

1959 AUSTIN MINI

The Mini was a triumph of innovative packaging by engineer Alec Issigonis. But more importantly, its cute looks seemed to fit perfectly with the fashions of the new "Swinging Sixties" in Britain. Well-known figures such as the Beatles, Princess Margaret, and Twiggy were soon spotted driving around London in the trendy new car, and its iconic status was established.

The nimble Mini beat bigger rivals to win international rallies.

37

1959 AUSTIN MINI

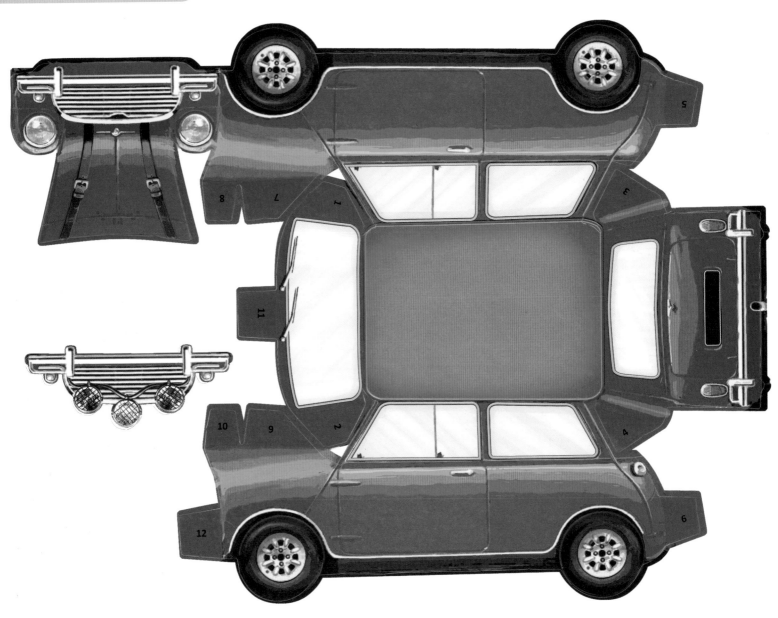

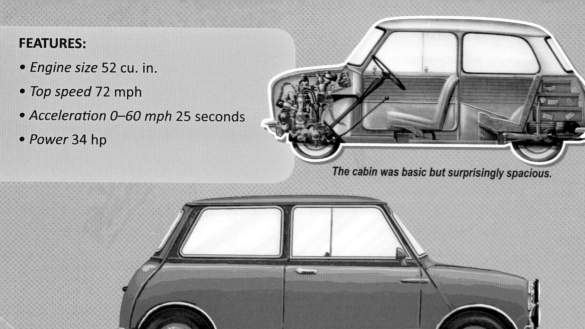

FEATURES:

- *Engine size* 52 cu. in.
- *Top speed* 72 mph
- *Acceleration 0–60 mph* 25 seconds
- *Power* 34 hp

The cabin was basic but surprisingly spacious.

AUSTIN MINI

The Mini's engine was positioned sideways instead of lengthwise, and powered the front wheels instead of the back wheels. This shortened the hood and freed 80 percent of the car's area for passengers and luggage. Small cars were never the same again.

1961 JAGUAR E-TYPE SERIES I

With its long hood, supercar performance, and glamorous modern lines, the E-Type was the 1960's dream car. The Jag attracted big-name owners such as soccer star George Best, singer Roy Orbison, and actors Steve McQueen and Tony Curtis—and made small boys drool whenever one roared past.

"The most beautiful car ever made," according to Enzo Ferrari. More than 70,000 were sold.

1961 JAGUAR E-TYPE SERIES I

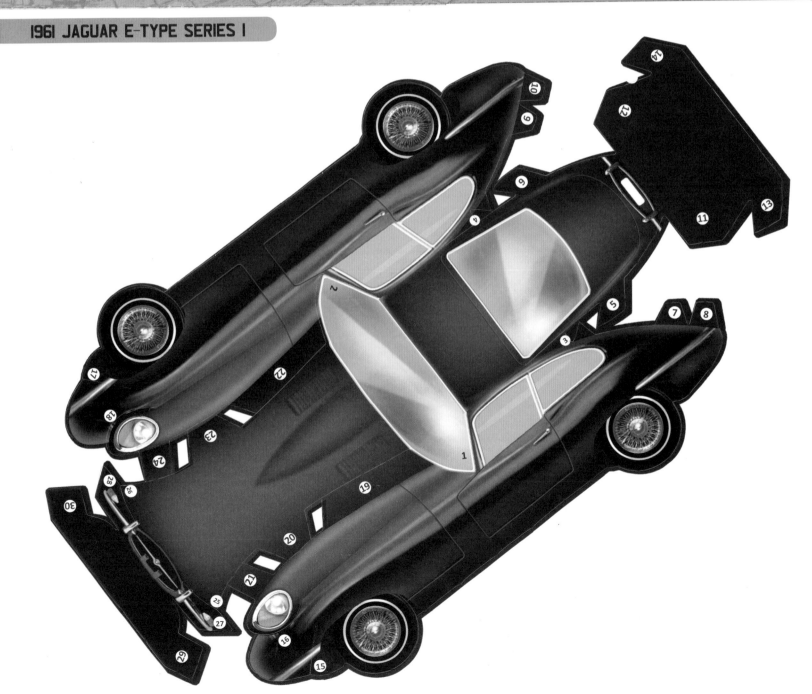

FEATURES:

- *Engine size* 231 cu. in.
- *Top speed* 153 mph
- *Acceleration 0–60 mph* 6.7 seconds
- *Power* 265 hp

JAGUAR E-TYPE SERIES 1

The E-Type's appeal was more to do with its looks and speed than its technical sophistication. The gearbox was only four-speed with no synchromesh for the first gear, which meant using an awkward de-clutching technique—but buyers didn't seem to mind.

The big engine dated back to the 1950s.

1962 FERRARI 250 GTO

Ferrari built GTOs simply to win track races, but also had to build 39 for sale to customers to conform to racing rules. No one thought these lightweight racers would turn into one of the world's most venerated objects, but once celebrities started collecting them, prices began to soar.

Only 39 250 GTOs were built. A rare 1963 model changed hands for $32 million in 2013.

41

1962 FERRARI 250 GTO

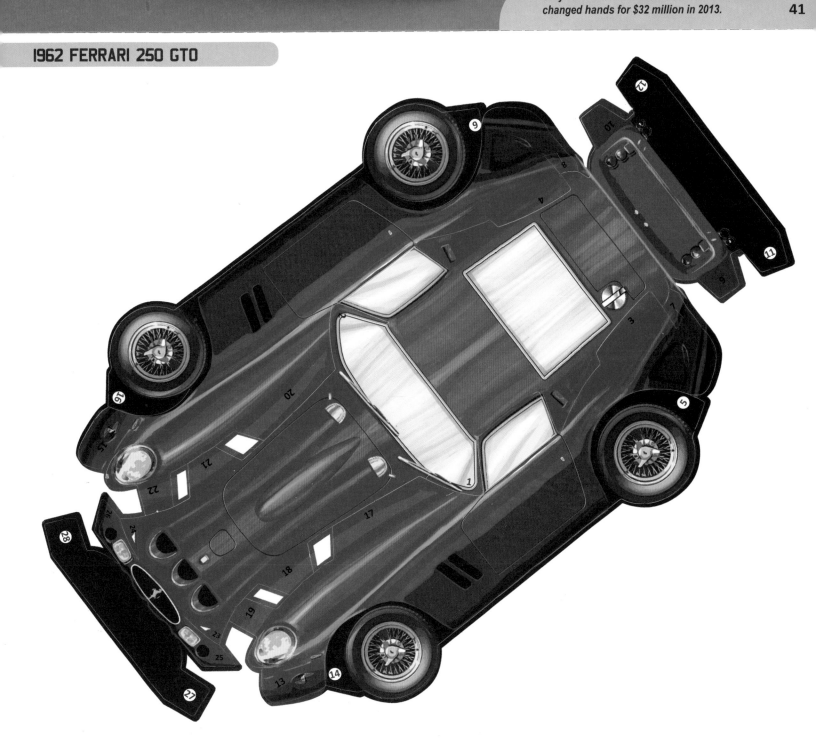

FEATURES:

- *Engine size* 180 cu. in.
- *Top speed* 176 mph
- *Acceleration 0–60 mph* 4.9 seconds
- *Power* 302 hp

The GTO's Borrani wire wheels were handmade in Milan.

FERRARI 250 GTO

Ferrari considered the GTO such a high-performance road car that all buyers had to be personally approved by Enzo himself. The model won the World GT Championship for three consecutive years, but it was one of the last racing cars to have its engine at the front. From here on, track car engines were normally positioned behind the driver.

1963 ASTON MARTIN DB5

This old-school British muscle car achieved iconic status as James Bond's car in the film *Goldfinger*. In one of the best-ever examples of product placement, Sean Connery's mix of charm, style, and thuggishness matched the DB5's beautiful coachwork, classic interior, and brutally muscular four-liter engine.

Bond's best-known car mixed Italian design with British tradition.

43

1963 ASTON MARTIN DB5

FEATURES:

- *Engine size* 244 cu. in.
- *Top speed* 142 mph
- *Acceleration 0–60 mph* 7.1 seconds
- *Power* 282 hp

ASTON MARTIN DB5

As 007's car, the DB5 received certain upgrades that were cemented in a generation's consciousness by the popular Corgi toy replica. Optional extras included a rocket-powered ejector passenger seat, wheel-mounted tire-slashers, bulletproof shield, radar scanner, machine guns, and rear smokescreen/oil-slick dispensers.

DB5s came with classic leather-and-wood cabins—but no ejector seat.

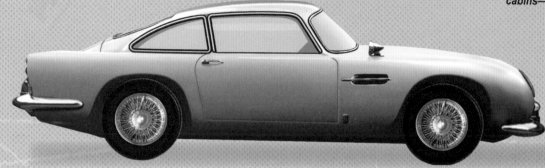

44

1963 PORSCHE 911

Porsche designed the VW Beetle, so perhaps it was no surprise that the car it began designing after World War II was launched with a similar bug-eyed curved body and an air-cooled engine in the back. But that's where the similarities ended, for this was a 131-mph machine with a distinctive character of its own.

The classic Porsche 911 sports car is still made today.

1963 PORSCHE 911

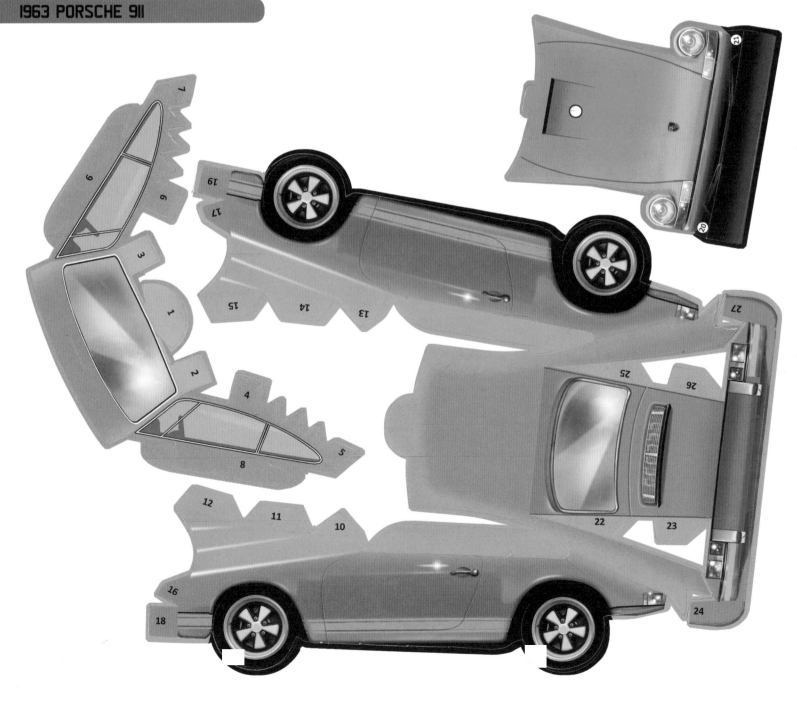

FEATURES:

- *Engine size* 121 cu. in.
- *Top speed* 131 mph
- *Acceleration 0–60 mph* 8.5 seconds
- *Power* 128 hp

PORSCHE 911

The familiar understated looks of the 911 belie a serious sports machine. For over 50 years the Porsche has been improved and developed while retaining its own style. The top 911 models are now 180-mph supercars but still use a similar "boxer" engine with six cylinders arranged in two opposing banks.

A 911 always has a rear engine.

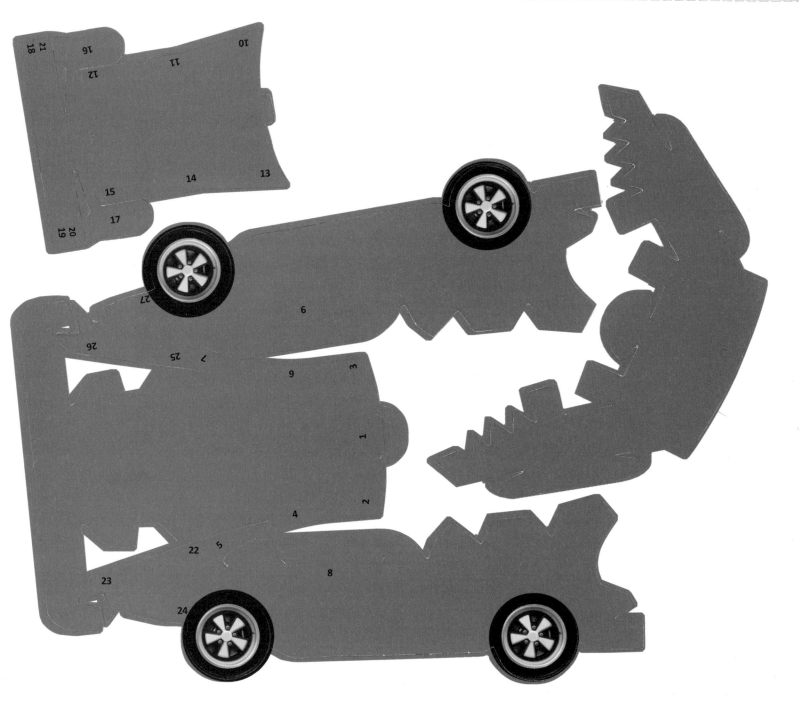

1963 AC CARS SHELBY COBRA

Give a classic English roadster to a Texas racing driver and what do you get? Le Mans winner Carroll Shelby transformed the AC Ace into a fire-breathing monster by persuading AC to install a big Ford V8 engine. This hot rod became a legendary performer on the road and track on both sides of the Atlantic.

A Cobra once drove at 186 mph on Britain's M1 motorway.

47

1963 AC CARS SHELBY COBRA

FEATURES:

- *Engine size* 260 cu. in.
- *Top speed* 143 mph
- *Acceleration 0–60 mph* 5.5 seconds
- *Power* 264 hp

The engine's at the front, but the Cobra has rear-wheel drive.

AC CARS SHELBY COBRA

The original AC Ace used a 156 cu. in. engine. Shelby swapped that for a 260 cu. in. unit, then 289 cu. in., and finally a monstrous 427 cu. in. V8 that allowed the little two-seater to reach a top speed of 186 mph on Britain's M1 motorway in 1964. A 70-mph national limit was introduced shortly afterward.

1964 FORD GT40

Ferrari had won the Le Mans 24-Hour race every year from 1960 to 1965. Henry Ford II realized what a promotional coup it would be if Ford could build a car to beat Ferrari. In 1966 he traveled to France to watch his new GT40s come first, second, and third. The car went on to win Le Mans for four consecutive years.

Henry Ford II watched as his GT40s won Le Mans in 1966.

1964 FORD GT40

FEATURES:

- *Engine size* 426 cu. in.
- *Top speed* 213 mph
- *Acceleration 0–60 mph* 4.2 seconds
- *Power* 485 hp

FORD GT40

The first American car to win at Le Mans was actually produced by a team of top engineers from Ford, Lola, and Aston Martin based in Slough, in England. The car they created had a lightweight fiberglass body and a big V8 engine mounted behind the driver but in front of the rear axle.

The GT40 dominated motorsport in the late 1960s.

1964 FORD MUSTANG MARK I

The Mustang, named after a World War II fighter plane, had purposeful, muscular styling that was uniquely exciting. The new Ford was an immediate success, selling a million in two years and launching a whole category of affordable sports coupés— America's "pony cars."

Steve McQueen's Mustang in Bullitt launched the "pony car" craze.

51

1964 FORD MUSTANG MARK I

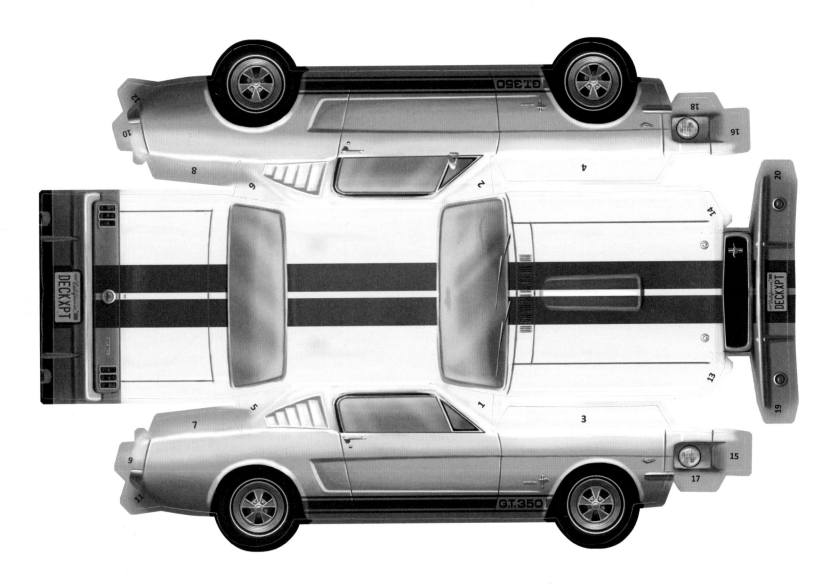

FEATURES:

- *Engine size* 301 cu. in.
- *Top speed* 116 mph
- *Acceleration 0–60 mph* 7.5 seconds
- *Power* 240 hp

FORD MUSTANG MARK 1

A car this cool was soon going to feature in popular culture. First came Wilson Pickett's hit single "Mustang Sally" in 1965, then the car was driven in one of the most acclaimed chases in film history by Steve McQueen in *Bullitt* in 1968. An assassin's Mustang even chased—and caught!—Bond's DB5 in the film *Goldfinger*.

McQueen tried in vain to buy the Mustang he drove in the film.

52

1967 CHEVROLET CORVETTE STINGRAY

Designers working on the second-generation Corvette were given two big styling cues: the rival Jaguar E-Type, and a shark once caught by one of GM's bosses. Somehow the Corvette team came up with a new car that combined elements of both—and their creation has often been acclaimed as one of the best-looking sports cars of its time.

The Stingray demanded high-octane racing fuel that was available only at select service stations.

53

1967 CHEVROLET CORVETTE STINGRAY

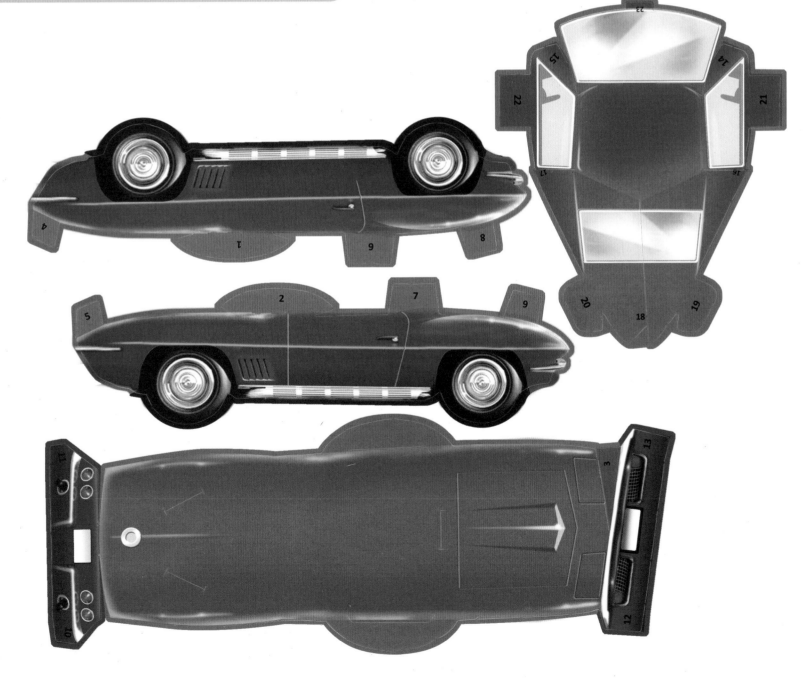

FEATURES:

- *Engine size* 327 cu. in.
- *Top speed* 147 mph
- *Acceleration 0–60 mph* 6.2 seconds
- *Power* 360 hp

Side exhaust pipes were stylish but dangerous.

CHEVROLET CORVETTE STINGRAY

In 1960's America, astronauts were the biggest stars around. General Motors' great marketing ploy was to give all the U.S. astronauts two cars: a "sensible" one for their wives and a Corvette each for themselves. Neil Armstrong had a 1967 Stingray, which was auctioned on eBay in 2012. It attracted bids of $250,000 before being withdrawn from sale.

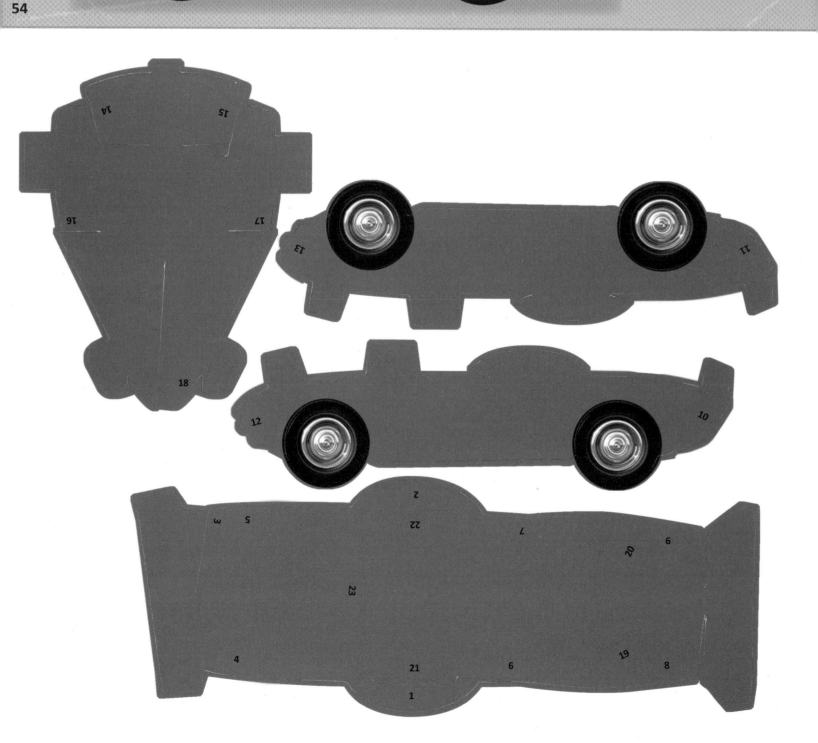

1969 FERRARI DINO 246

The Dino was Ferrari's attempt to create a budget rival to Porsche's popular 911. Enzo Ferrari was so worried that such a lowly machine with a mere V6 engine would damage his lofty reputation that he wouldn't even put Ferrari badges on it. The company's first mid-engined car, however, was widely acclaimed for its looks, handling, and performance.

It may have been the "budget" Ferrari, but it still had a top speed of 146 mph.

55

1969 FERRARI DINO 246

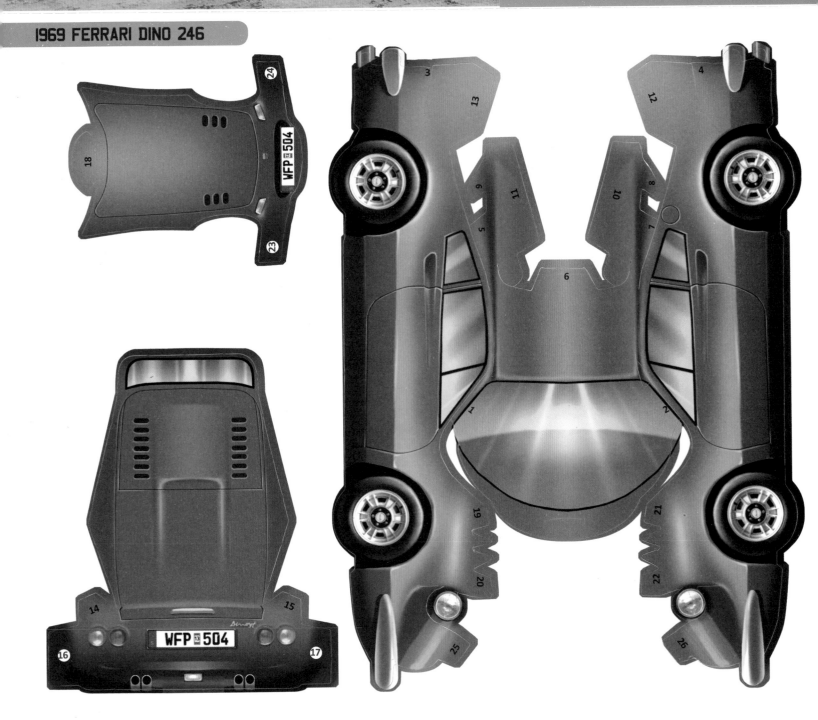

FEATURES:

- *Engine size* 147 cu. in.
- *Top speed* 146 mph
- *Acceleration 0–60 mph* 7.1 seconds
- *Power* 197 hp

FERRARI DINO 246

The Dino was named after Enzo Ferrari's son Dino, who designed the V6 engine. Sadly, Dino died of muscular dystrophy, aged just 24, before the car was launched. It might have been cheaper than most Ferraris but was chosen by many rich and famous owners, including race driver Mario Andretti.

The 246 used a six-cylinder engine instead of one of Ferrari's more powerful V12s.

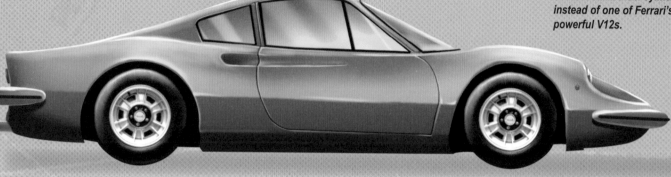

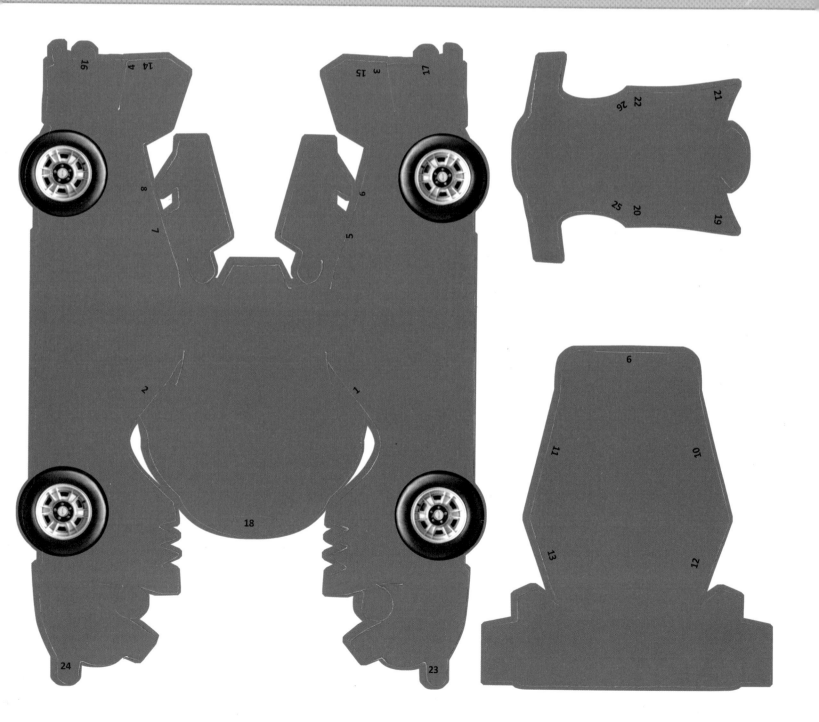

1969 PONTIAC GTO

They called them "muscle cars": medium-sized two-door coupés with huge V8 engines, tuned to produce tire-squealing acceleration. Pontiac's GTO was the king of these macho street-racers, with its fat tires, bulging curves, and menacing hood air scoops.

The GTO was cheap, it was cool, and it went fast in a straight line. That was enough to make young Americans drool.

1969 PONTIAC GTO

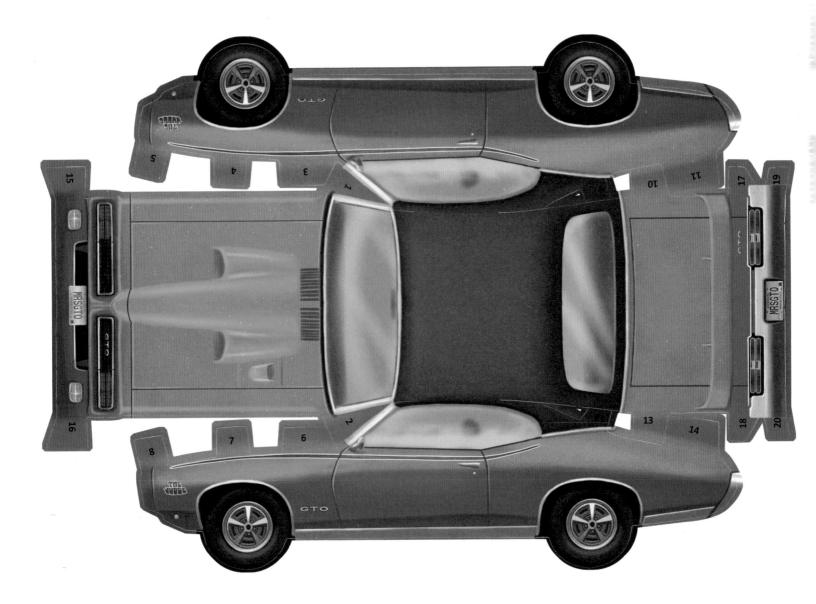

FEATURES:

- *Engine size* 400 cu. in.
- *Top speed* 124 mph
- *Acceleration 0–60 mph* 6.2 seconds
- *Power* 370 hp

Some GTOs featured a hood-mounted rev counter.

PONTIAC GTO

The 1969 GTO came in a famous special edition that became a cult classic. It was called "the Judge," after an irreverent and mischievous TV comedy catchphrase, "here come da judge." The GTO Judge came in bright colors, had a rear spoiler and lots of decals, but it was essentially the normal GTO underneath.

58

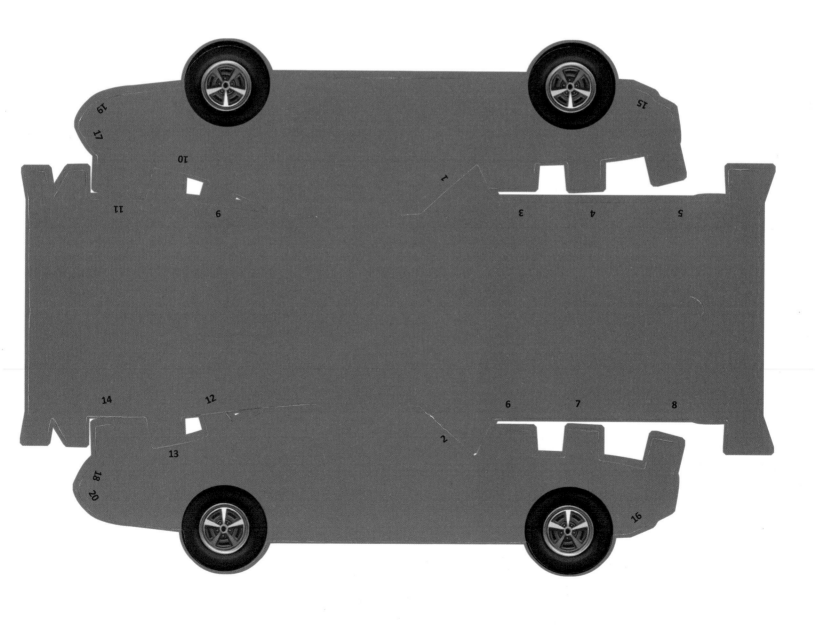

Legend has it that when the Lamborghini design boss saw the first drawings of the new car, "Countach!" is what he shouted. It's an exclamation in the local Piedmont dialect, traditionally made by men when they see a beautiful woman. The name stuck, and the striking new Lamborghini pioneered a new design style that supercars would follow for decades.

The Countach was the first wedge-shaped mid-engined supercar.

59

1974 LAMBORGHINI COUNTACH

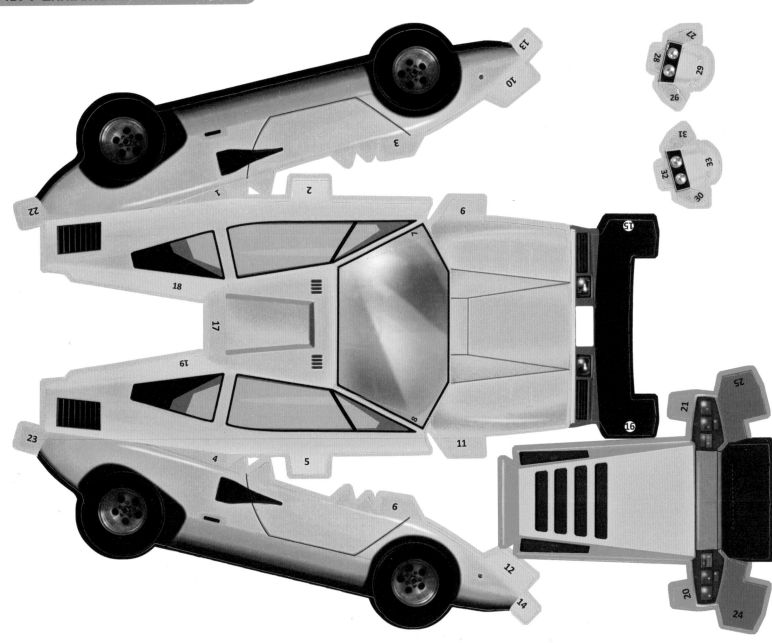

FEATURES:

- *Engine size* 315 cu. in.
- *Top speed* 185 mph
- *Acceleration 0–60 mph* 4.9 seconds
- *Power* 449 hp

LAMBORGHINI COUNTACH

By the mid-1980s the Countach had evolved to become even more spectacular, with a huge rear spoiler and the world's widest rear tires. And it was even faster: at 185 mph, it was the fastest production road car of 1975, which is why it adorned countless teenagers' bedroom walls around the world.

Curves were old news: abrupt angles had become cool.

60

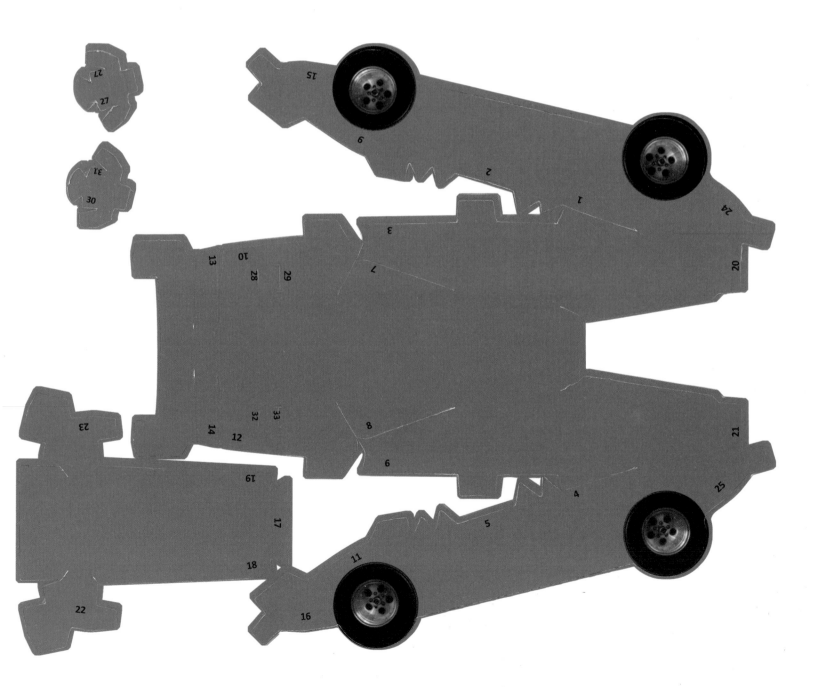

1976 GM HOLDEN UTE HX

The "Ute" was the nickname Australians gave the post-war Holden Coupé Utility pickup truck. It became, and remains, an established part of rural life. The HX version of 1976 was part of the move to bigger engines. "The best partner a working man can have," ran the slogan.

The Ute's practicality suited the outdoor lifestyle Down Under.

61

1976 GM HOLDEN UTE HX

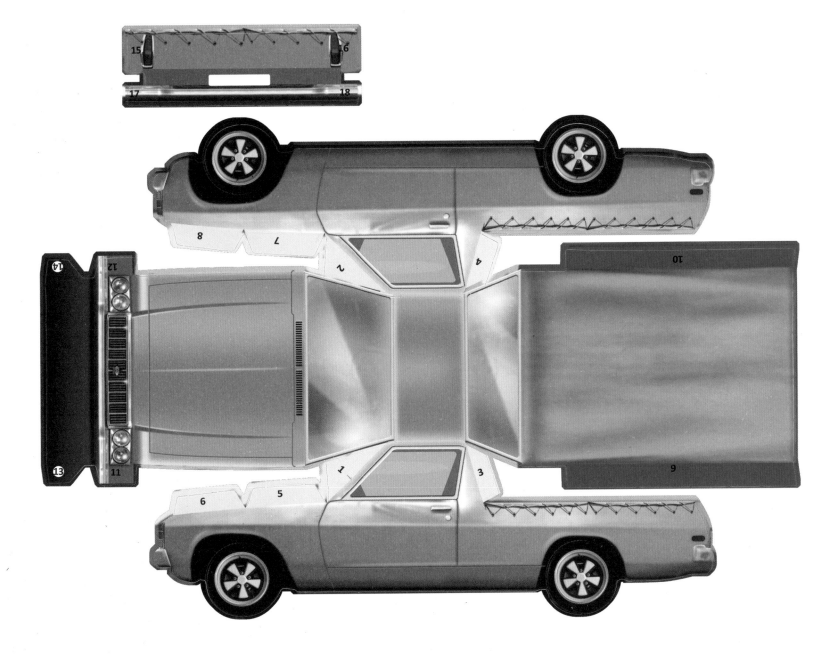

FEATURES:

- *Engine size* 308 cu. in.
- *Top speed* Unknown
- *Acceleration 0–60 mph* 10.2 seconds
- *Power* 216 hp

Hot-rodded Utes could burn rubber like sports cars.

GM HOLDEN UTE HX

The '76 Ute had unsophisticated two-wheel-drive underpinnings with a chunky steel chassis and a rugged three-liter, six-cylinder engine. But some buyers opted for a huge five-liter V8 instead. Other options included bucket seats, rally wheels, and a sports dashboard. Many preferred to customize their Ute themselves, often turning them into hot-rod-style pickups with sports car performance.

62

1977 PONTIAC FIREBIRD TRANS AM

Pontiac's muscle car had been around since 1967 and had looked much the same for the previous seven years before it appeared in the hit film *Smokey and the Bandit*. After hero Burt Reynolds jumped the black-and-gold Firebird across broken bridges, drifted around corners, and evaded the hapless police, suddenly everyone in America wanted one, and sales soared.

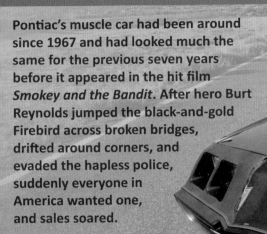

America's flashiest muscle car benefited from film and TV exposure.

63

1977 PONTIAC FIREBIRD TRANS AM

FEATURES:

- *Engine size* 400 cu. in.
- *Top speed* 131 mph
- *Acceleration 0–60 mph* 9.3 seconds
- *Power* 180 hp

PONTIAC FIREBIRD TRANS AM

The Pontiac pony car starred in a big TV series, too—as the talking super-robot car KITT in *Knight Rider* in 1982. David Hasselhoff's character Michael Knight drove the high-tech Firebird to chase serious criminals, including KITT's evil adversary: another Firebird called KARR. The series ran for four years.

Burt Reynolds became a star and so did the Firebird.

64

1980 AUDI QUATTRO

The Quattro brought sophisticated rally-bred four-wheel-drive and turbocharging to the road. This fast two-door coupé became a such a popular symbol of the 1980s, it featured on a UK Labour Party 2010 election poster asking voters not to go "back to the eighties." The Conservative Party replied with the same poster but saying: "Fire up the Quattro. It's time for change." The Conservatives won.

By powering all four wheels, the Quattro could dominate rallying.

65

1980 AUDI QUATTRO

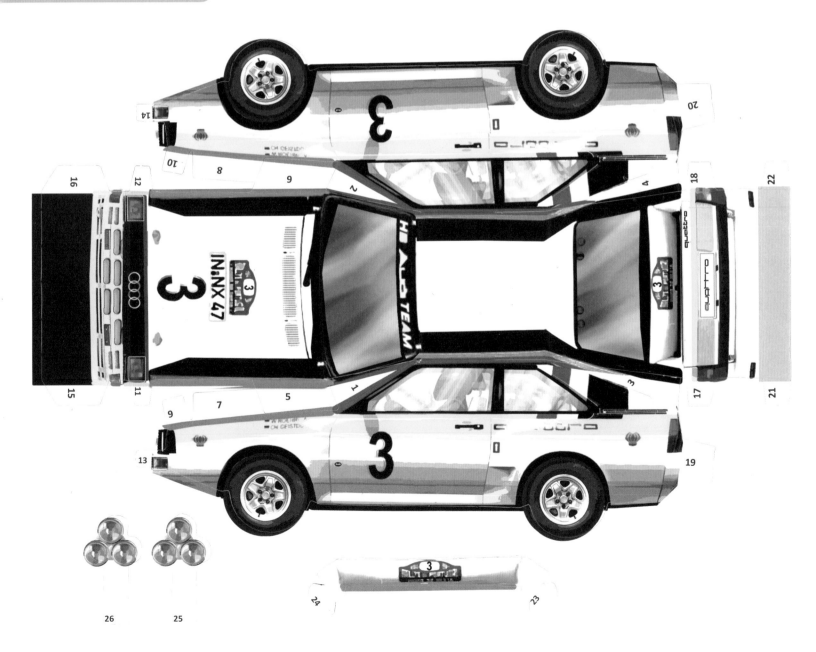

FEATURES:

- *Engine size* 131 cu. in.
- *Top speed* 143 mph
- *Acceleration 0–60 mph* 6.9 seconds
- *Power* 197 hp

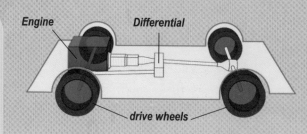

Engine   **Differential**

drive wheels

Audi was the first to offer a mass-produced road car with all-wheel drive.

AUDI QUATTRO

Audi now uses the word *Quattro*—"four" in Italian—on any models that feature four-wheel drive. It wasn't a new idea in 1980: military and agricultural vehicles were already sending power to all four wheels instead of the normal two to increase grip in difficult terrain.

66

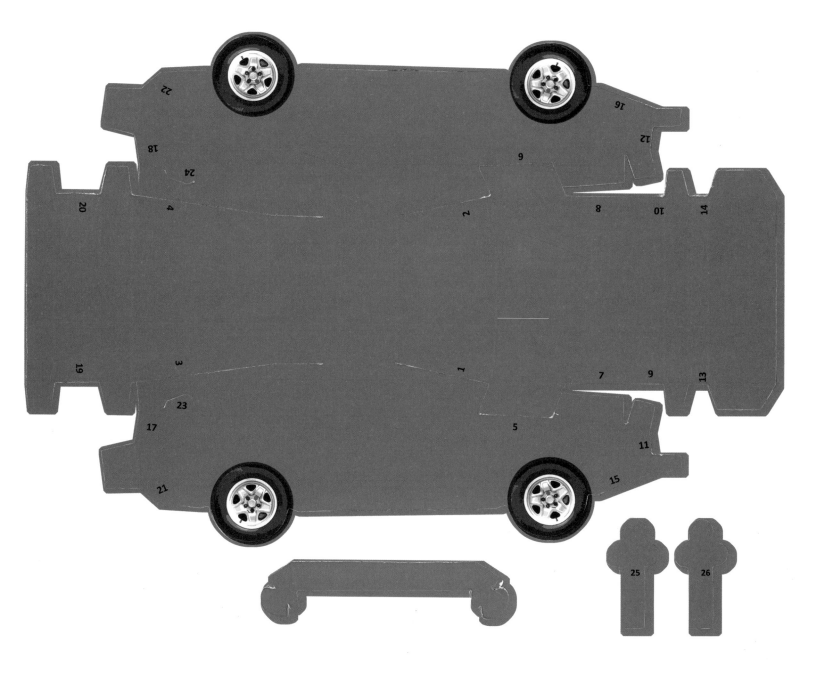

1981 DELOREAN DMC

Former GM boss John DeLorean's pet project was a sensational-looking sports coupé with gull-wing doors and unpainted body. The American's ambitious car was to be built in Northern Ireland but was defeated by financial, political, and reliability problems.

The DeLorean was immortalized as the time-travel machine in the Back to the Future films.

1981 DELOREAN DMC

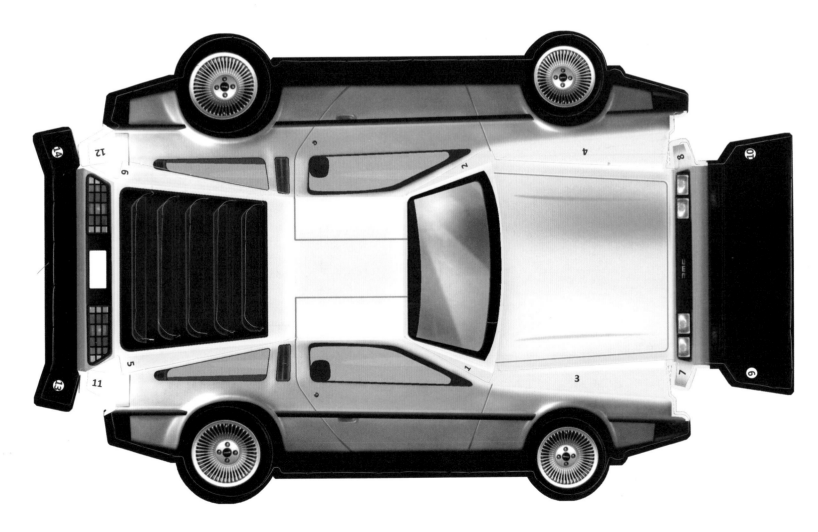

FEATURES:

- *Engine size* 173 cu. in.
- *Top speed* 110 mph
- *Acceleration 0–60 mph* 8.8 seconds
- *Power* 156 hp

DELOREAN DMC

The DeLorean was styled by acclaimed Italian designer Giorgetto Giugaro, with engineering help from Colin Chapman of Lotus. The innovative car featured a rear-mounted engine, a fiberglass underbody, and brushed stainless-steel panels. Performance was a little underwhelming, however, especially for the American market, where cars were restricted to 130 hp by emission regulations.

The films were too late to help DMC sales.

68

1990 HONDA NSX

Japan's first supercar was hand-built by 200 specially picked engineers. Its handling was fine-tuned by test drivers from Formula 1. Actor Harvey Keitel drove one in the cult movie *Pulp Fiction*, remarking dryly as he drove off: "That's thirty minutes away. I'll be there in ten."

The NSX showed the West that Japan could build supercars, too.

69

1990 HONDA NSX

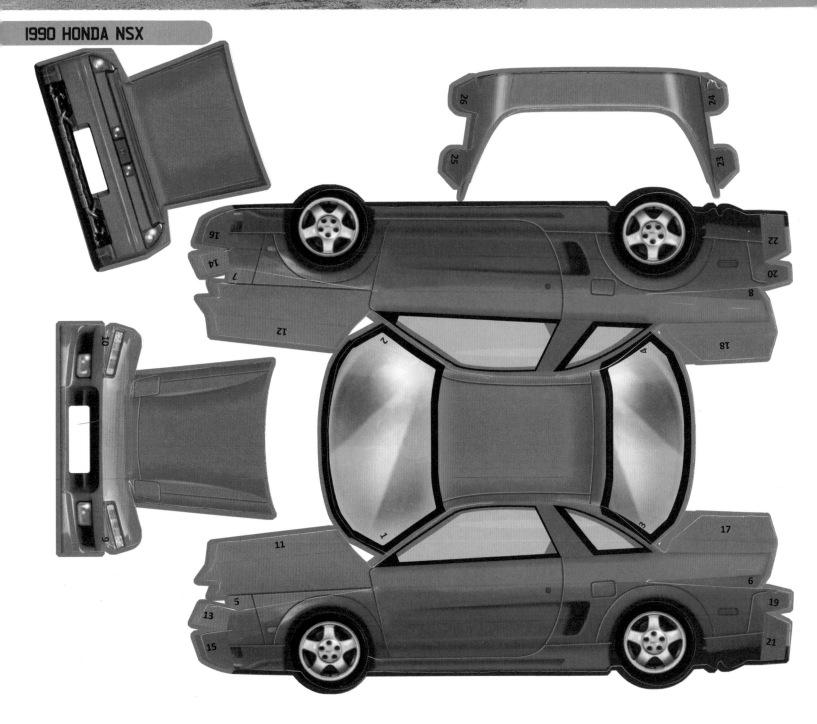

HONDA NSX

FEATURES:
- *Engine size* 194 cu. in.
- *Top speed* 168 mph
- *Acceleration 0–60 mph* 4.4 seconds
- *Power* 276 hp

The NSX was the first production car to be built entirely of aluminum, right down to the state-of-the-art VTEC variable-valve-timing V6 engine and clever double-wishbone suspension. Its mid-engine, rear-wheel-drive layout combined with use of lightweight, noncorrosive metal meant the NSX was not only fast, but also handled with precision and balance.

Japanese police use an NSX for highway patrols.

1992 CHRYSLER DODGE VIPER

Dodge put a monstrous eight-liter V10 engine in an open-top two-seater made of fiberglass panels. There were no driver aids such as traction control or antilock brakes, nor any creature comforts such as a roof, side windows, airbags, or external door handles. The result is one of the most visceral driving experiences, full of noise, speed, and excitement.

Viper buyers were eventually offered the luxury of a roof.

71

1992 CHRYSLER DODGE VIPER

FEATURES:

- *Engine size* 488 cu. in.
- *Top speed* 180 mph
- *Acceleration 0–60 mph* 4.6 seconds
- *Power* 400 hp

The big engine came from a truck.

CHRYSLER DODGE VIPER

The cast-iron Chrysler truck engine was remade in aluminum to reduce weight, but it was still bigger than two E-Type Jaguar engines. It was a crude design, lacking the multivalve and overhead camshaft technology of even an average hatchback, but it compensated with its enormous cubic capacity. This gave the car an instant power thrust at any speed.

1992 MCLAREN F1

When a Formula 1 team builds a road car, it's bound to be fast, sophisticated, and eye-wateringly expensive. The F1 was the world's fastest car and, at $960,000, the most expensive. When Rowan "Mr. Bean" Atkinson crashed his F1 into a tree in 2011, the insurance repair claim was one of the biggest ever—almost $1.5 million.

McLaren F1 drivers sit in the middle. Passengers sit behind.

73

1992 MCLAREN F1

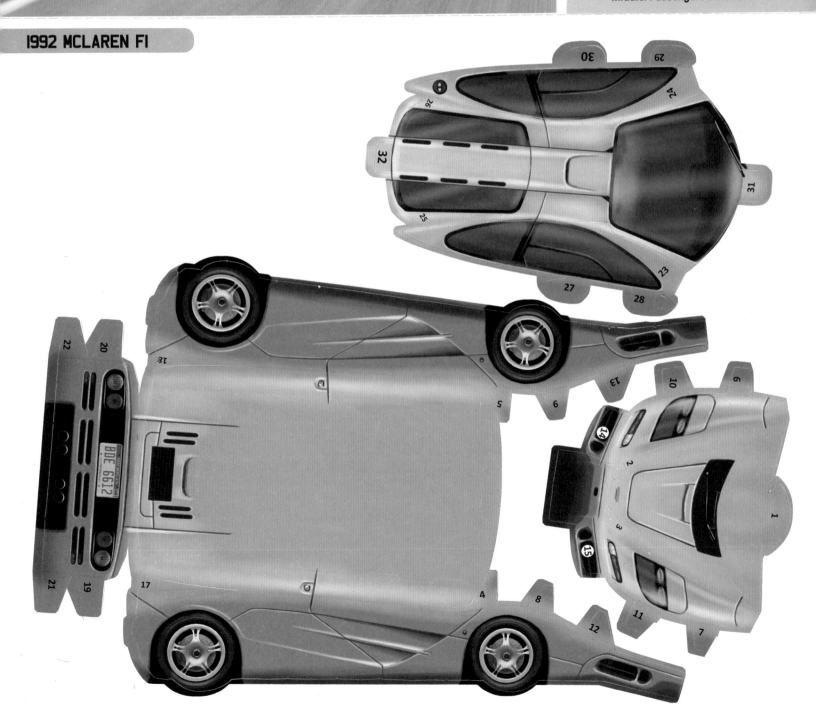

FEATURES:

- *Engine size* 370 cu. in.
- *Top speed* 241 mph
- *Acceleration 0–60 mph* 3.1 seconds
- *Power* 618 hp

Scissor doors swivel upward and forward.

MCLAREN F1

Everything about the F1 was special, from the materials used (plastic, titanium, magnesium, gold, Kevlar, and carbon) to the seating arrangement. The doors opened by being slid forward and upward, and the spoiler and air intakes automatically adjusted to the speed. Custom luggage bags were even included; they fit exactly into each of the cargo compartments.

1992 GENERAL MOTORS HUMMER HI

USA

For a while the Hummer became the coolest boulevard cruiser in America. It was like driving a big cumbersome truck with a cramped, noisy, and basic cabin, but buyers loved its unstoppable image. If necessary, it could climb up a step almost two feet high and drive through 30 inches of water.

The giant off-roader was originally used by the U.S. Army.

75

1992 GENERAL MOTORS HUMMER HI

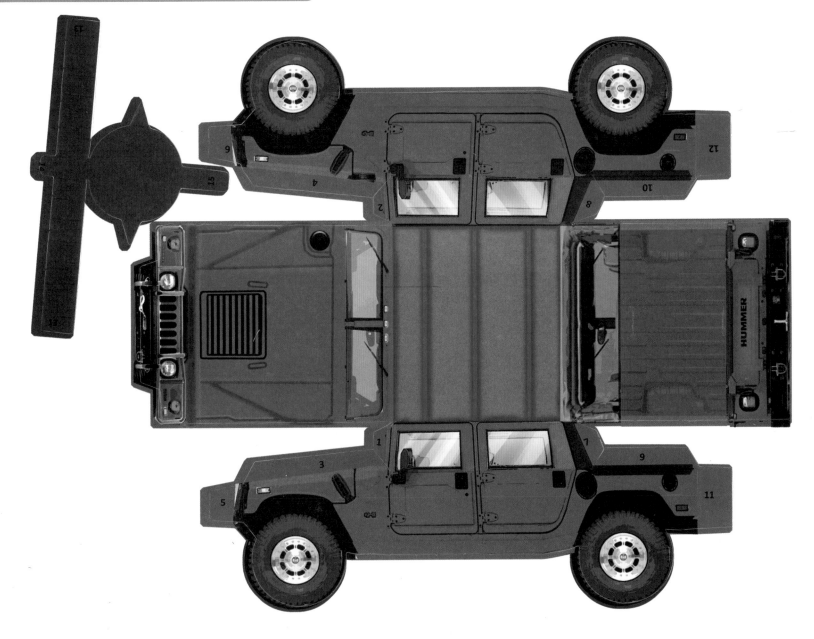

FEATURES:

- *Engine size* 397 cu. in.
- *Top speed* 83 mph
- *Acceleration 0–60 mph* 17.8 seconds
- *Power* 194 hp

The 3.5-ton Hummer dwarfs other road cars.

GM HUMMER H1

After the Gulf War in 1991, actor Arnold Schwarzenegger campaigned for the distinctive military Humvee to be produced for civilians too. It was called "a mechanical symbol of freedom." Arnie succeeded and bought the first two Hummers built.

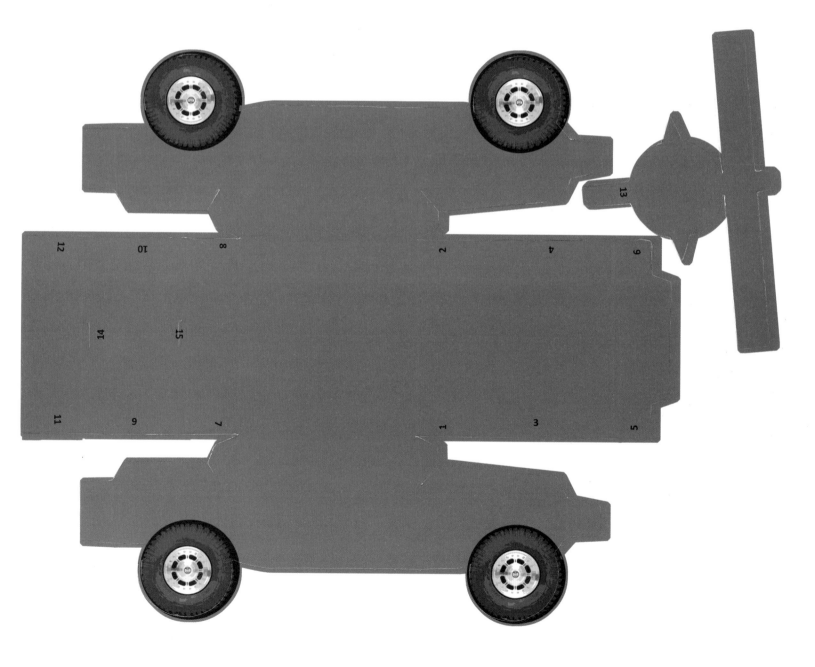

1997 TOYOTA PRIUS

The Prius was the first hybrid production car—and a symbol of manufacturers' and drivers' growing environmental awareness. It used less fuel and created less pollution than gas-only cars because at slow speeds it was propelled by an emission-free electric motor. The gas engine fired up only when additional power was needed, and to help recharge the batteries.

The first popular hybrid has become a favorite of Hollywood stars.

77

1997 TOYOTA PRIUS

FEATURES:

- *Engine size* 91 cu. in.
- *Top speed* 99 mph
- *Acceleration 0–60 mph* 12.7 seconds
- *Power* 58 hp

TOYOTA PRIUS

Despite its very average performance, features, and looks, the Prius's green image has attracted a flood of high-profile celebrity owners. A fleet of Priuses have also been used as "limousines" at the glamorous Academy Awards ceremony.

The Prius has a recharging socket to connect an electrical cable.

78

1998 AUDI TT

Audi had gradually transformed itself into one of the most fashionable brands by the time it launched this cutely curvaceous two-seater. It was available as a coupé or convertible with a selection of sporty engines and even a Quattro four-wheel-drive system. It was judged Design Car of the Year.

The sleek curved body made the TT a new fashion icon.

79

1998 AUDI TT

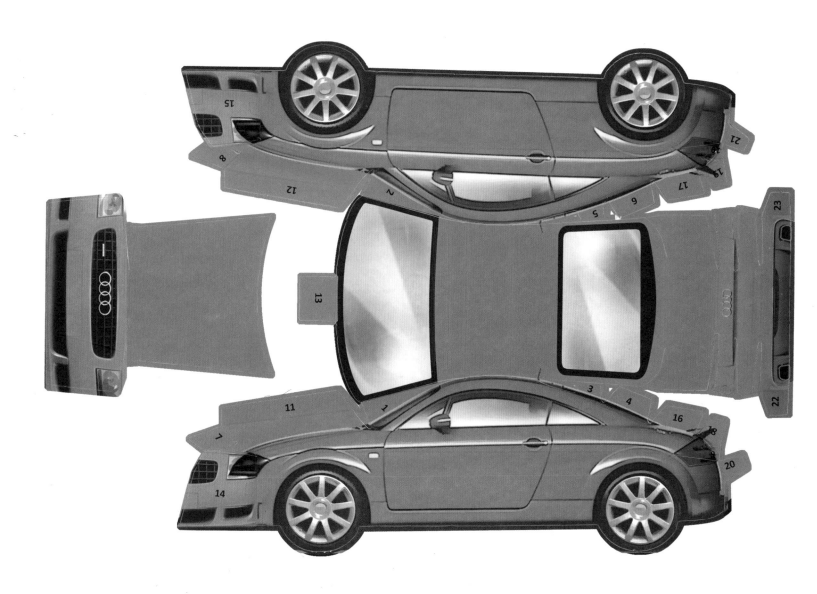

FEATURES:

- *Engine size* 151 cu. in.
- *Top speed* 155 mph
- *Acceleration 0–60 mph* 4.6 seconds
- *Power* 335 hp

With the TT, Audi cemented its reputation for hi-tech cars.

AUDI TT

The TT shows how skilled modern manufacturers have become at working from a single mechanical framework. It was based on a Volkswagen Group platform, which meant it shared its floorpan, suspension, steering, axles, and mechanical layout with cars as different as the VW Golf, Skoda Octavia, and Seat Leon.

1999 BMW Z8

BMW's roadster was styled like a retro classic but used the sophisticated 32-valve V8 engine from the M5 super-saloon. The Z8 also featured unique neon lights and a minimalist interior that hid air-conditioning, sat-nav, and stereo controls behind panels.

The modern lightweight aluminum chassis belied the vintage styling.

1999 BMW Z8

FEATURES:

- *Engine size* 302 cu. in.
- *Top speed* 155 mph
- *Acceleration 0–60 mph* 4.8 seconds
- *Power* 400 hp

Retracting panels help preserve the interior's vintage simplicity.

BMW Z8

In *The World Is Not Enough*, Pierce Brosnan's James Bond drove a Z8 that had side-mounted rocket-launchers and could be remotely controlled using the key fob. Sadly, it ended up sliced in half by a tree-cutting helicopter. As 007 stepped from the wreckage, immaculate in a dinner suit, he remarked dryly, "Q is not going to like this."

82

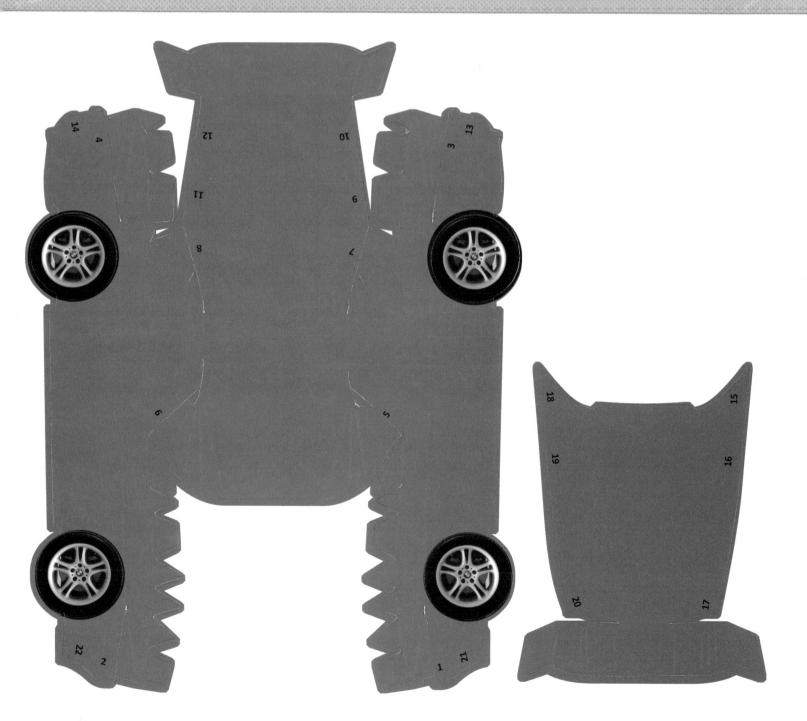

2005 SUBURU IMPREZA

This range of small Japanese saloons and hatchbacks that have been on sale since 1992 are remarkable only for being well built and reliable. Apart from the four-wheel-drive, turbocharged version, that is. This WRX model with its menacing hood air-scoop and big tail spoiler was a fire-breathing rally car for road drivers.

Top rally editions of the humble Impreza are mini supercars.

2005 SUBURU IMPREZA

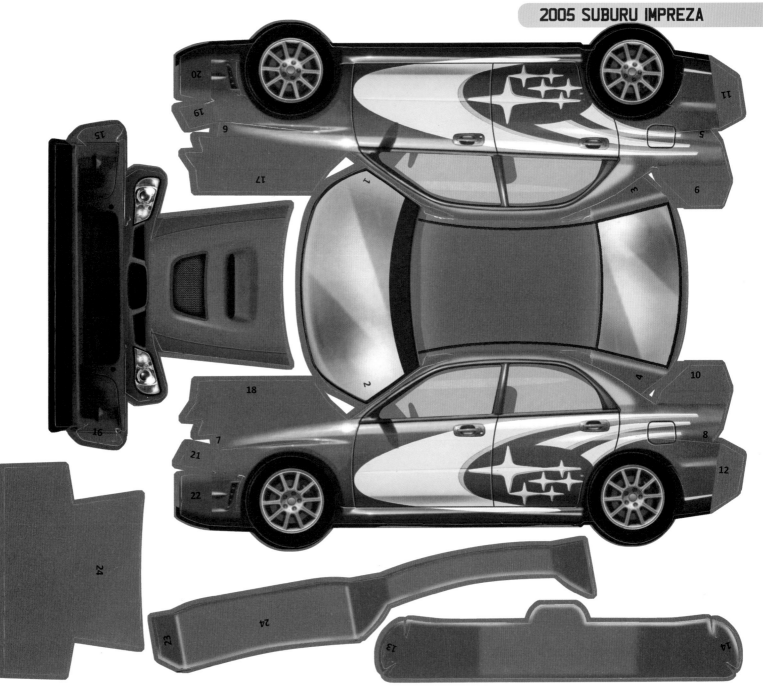

FEATURES:

- *Engine size* 150 cu. in.
- *Top speed* 158 mph
- *Acceleration 0–60 mph* 5.4 seconds
- *Power* 280 hp

Petter Solberg won the driver's world rally title in an Impreza.

SUBARU IMPREZA

The WRX 2.5 STI Turbo was top of the range. All the Imprezas have a "flat-four" engine with horizontally opposed pairs of cylinders. In the WRX STI this was a specially tuned 16-valve multipoint injection unit with a turbocharger and all-wheel drive. Rally extras included projector beam fog lights and wider rear wheels with flared wheel arches.

2005 BUGATTI VEYRON

It's one of the most famous supercars ever made: a mid-engined, four-wheel-drive, two-door coupé costing $1,300,000 that reaches higher top speeds than any other road car. It's an over-the-top, money-no-object status symbol created when VW took over the dormant Bugatti brand.

The Veyron's brazen image suits glamorous celebrity owners, including soccer and TV stars.

85

2005 BUGATTI VEYRON

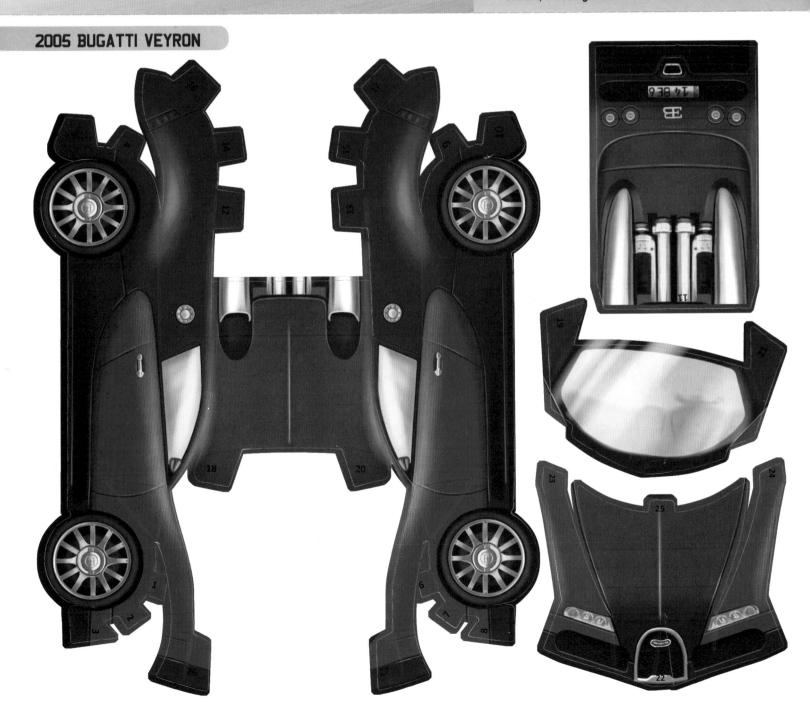

FEATURES:

- *Engine size* 488 cu. in.
- *Top speed* 254 mph
- *Acceleration 0–60 mph* 2.5 seconds
- *Power* 987 hp

BUGATTI VEYRON

The Veyron's features are mind-boggling: the 16-cylinder engine has four turbochargers and 64 valves. There are ten radiators, and special Michelin tires costing $25,000 per set—plus extra to fit. At top speed it manages only around three miles per gallon.

The auto gearbox shifts gears in 150 milliseconds.

86

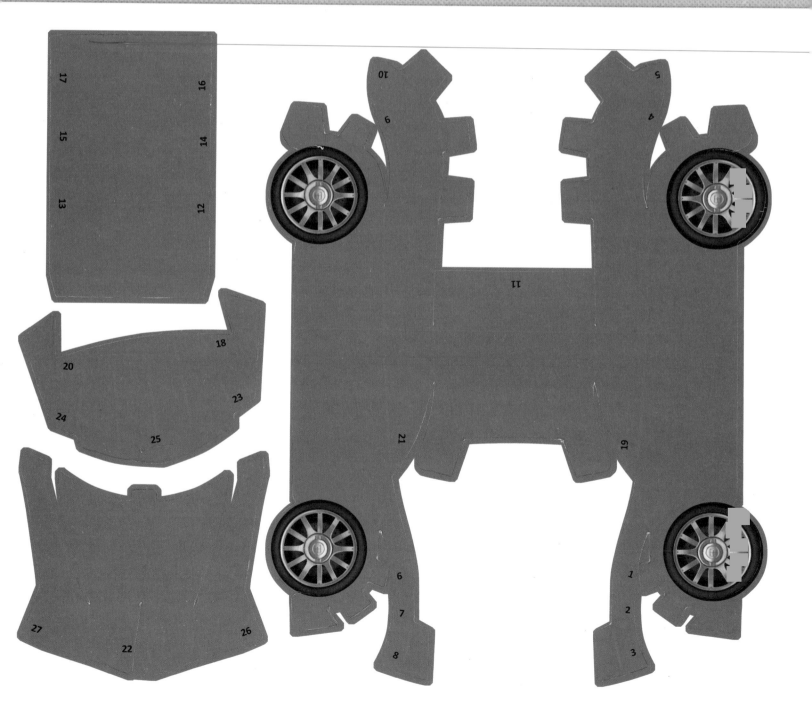

In its four years of production, apparently only 14 CCXs were sold, but that's hardly a problem for a manufacturer when each car costs up to $4,850,000. That's the price of the top CCX model, the Trevita, which has a body impregnated with diamonds and is the world's most expensive street-legal production car.

VD·565·985

The 250-mph Koenigsegg can run on fuel made from potatoes.

FEATURES:

- *Engine size* 287 cu. in.
- *Top speed* 250 mph
- *Acceleration 0–60 mph* 2.9 seconds
- *Power* 795 hp

"Butterfly" doors add glamour to the world's priciest car.

KOENIGSEGG CCX

The mid-mounted engine has twin superchargers and enormous power but can be ordered so that it runs on the "green" fuel ethanol. Like a racing car, the CCX's body is made of lightweight carbon fiber, Kevlar, and aluminum. Even the wheels and brakes are carbon.

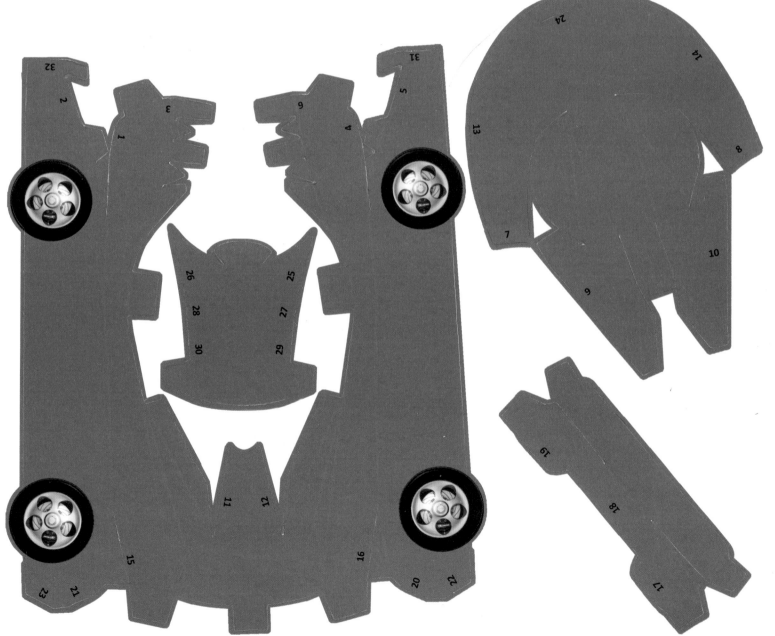

2007 AUDI R8

It seemed unlikely that the maker of A3 hatchbacks could create a machine such as this until you remember that Audi had taken over Lamborghini nine years earlier. In fact, the R8's underpinnings were shared with those of the Gallardo, but it had a more purposeful Audi-style aluminum body on top, a mid-mounted Audi V8 engine, and Quattro four-wheel-drive system.

Iron Man's wheels: the R8 is Audi's first supercar.

89

FEATURES:

- *Engine size* 256 cu. in.
- *Top speed* 188 mph
- *Acceleration 0–60 mph* 4.6 seconds
- *Power* 414 hp

AUDI R8

The most famous R8 owner is surely businessman and inventor Tony Stark, who drove an R8 in the film *Iron Man*. Stark switched to the R8 Spyder for the follow-up film and then drove the electric-powered R8 E-Tron for 2013's *Iron Man III*.

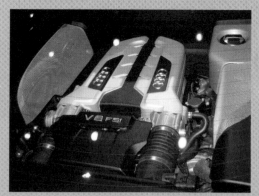
A special rear window shows off the R8's engine.

2008 DAIMLER SMART FORTWO

The innovative micro-car was a collaboration between funky watchmaker Swatch and conservative car builder Mercedes. Swatch dropped out before the ForTwo was launched, but its design input ensured the two-seater looked cool and modern.

The Smart car won over city drivers who valued the ease of parking and futuristic feel.

91

2008 DAIMLER SMART FORTWO

FEATURES:

- *Engine size* 61 cu. in.
- *Top speed* 92 mph
- *Acceleration 0–60 mph* 13.8 seconds
- *Power* 84 hp

DAIMLER SMART FORTWO

The Smart was surprisingly unusual underneath, too. There was a small three-cylinder turbocharged engine in the back and all versions had a semiautomatic gearbox. Sportier versions soon appeared, including a Brabus-tuned Crossblade cabrio model.

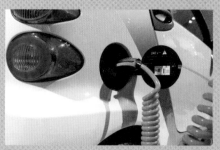

Buyers can opt for a plug-in electric version.

The car is sold in glass "vending machines."

2009 CADILLAC ONE

It cost $300,000 to build the American president's latest limousine. "Cadillac One," or "the Beast" as it's known within the White House, is based on a Cadillac STS with a big, powerful diesel engine, but has been transformed with such heavy-duty security features that it has been called "the tank that looks like a car."

Night-vision cameras and tear-gas canisters are secreted in the front bumper.

93

2009 CADILLAC ONE

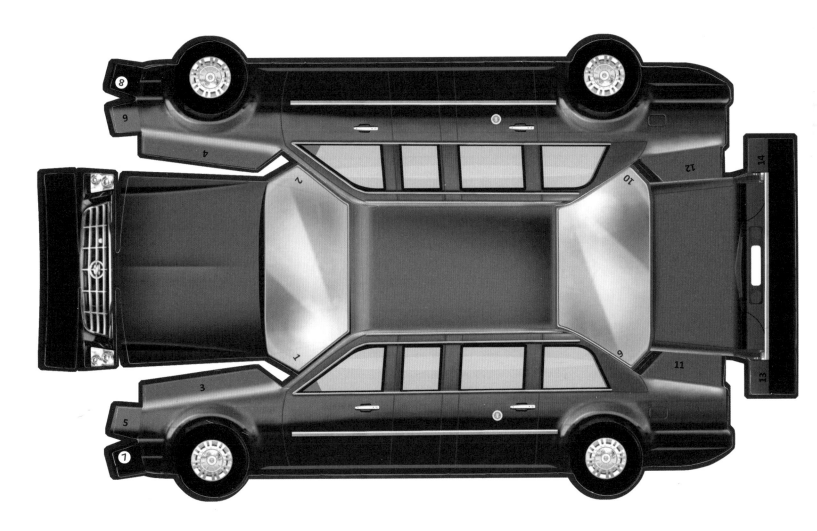

FEATURES:

- *Engine size* 397 cu. in.
- *Top speed* 60 mph
- *Acceleration 0–60 mph* 15 seconds
- *Power* Unknown

CADILLAC ONE

The Cadillac One features eight-inch-thick armor plating to stop rocket-propelled grenades, and a bombproof five-inch steel plate underneath. The rear compartment windows don't open, so it's sealed against a chemical attack, and it has its own oxygen supply.

The windows are bulletproof.

94

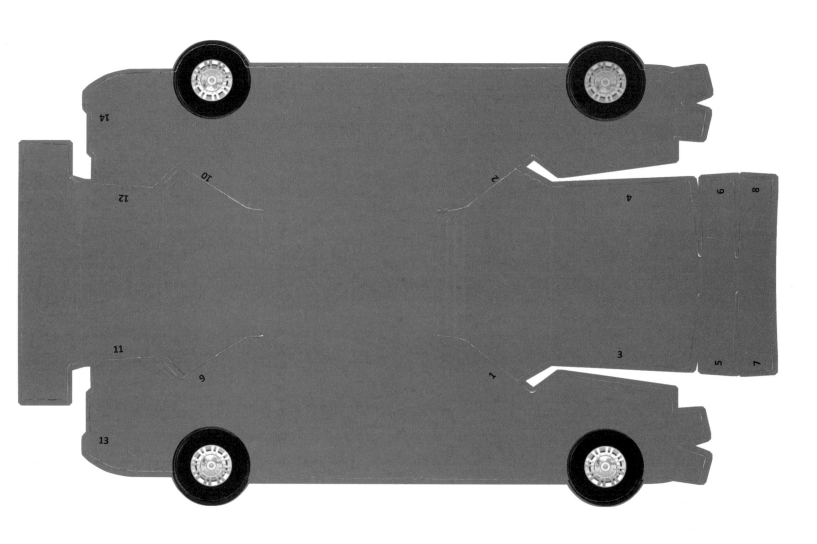

2010 MERCEDES SLS AMG

With gull-wing doors opening on powered struts, the SLS was deliberately evocative of historic Mercedes models. But the underpinnings were up-to-date: a handmade aluminum chassis with variable settings and a muscular V8 driving through a seven-speed semiautomatic gearbox. The wheels and body are aluminum, too.

The SLS is built by high-performance specialists at AMG.

2010 MERCEDES SLS AMG

FEATURES:
- *Engine size* 379 cu. in.
- *Top speed* 197 mph
- *Acceleration 0–60 mph* 3.8 seconds
- *Power* 563 hp

Gull-wing doors are a retro touch.

MERCEDES SLS AMG
A British TV ad for the roadster version showed racing driver David Coulthard driving an SLS so fast it catches a speeding golf ball. The car was also made famous as the track safety car in the 2010 Formula 1 season.

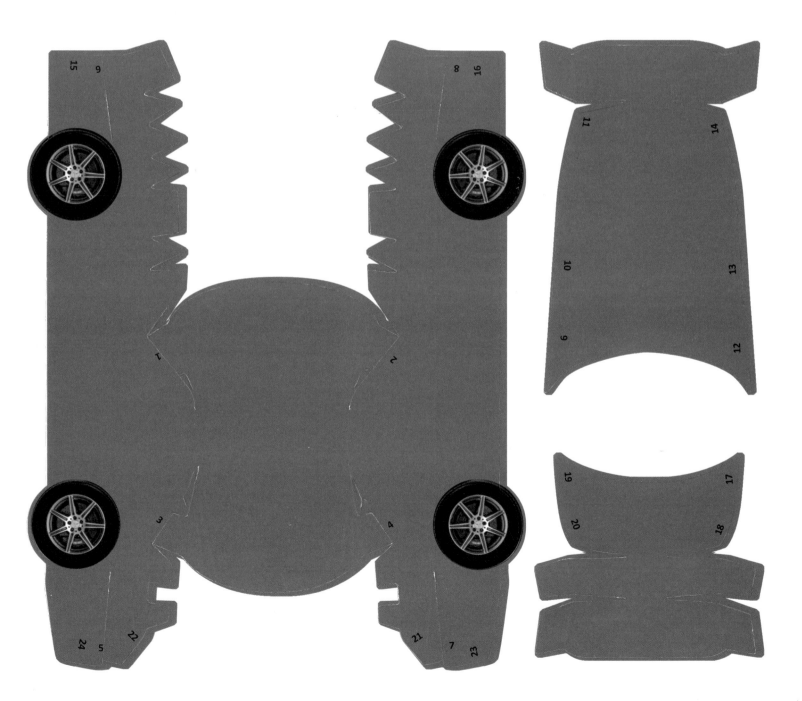

Lamborghini knew that its super-fast, rear-mounted, alloy V12 engine was the most attractive feature of this new car—so it placed a window in the body above the engine to put it on display. That 691-hp technical marvel powers the car through a four-wheel-drive system supplied by Audi.

The body is designed with gaping air scoops to cool the brakes and engine.

97

2011 LAMBORGHINI AVENTADOR

FEATURES:

- *Engine size* 397 cu. in.
- *Top speed* 217 mph
- *Acceleration 0–60 mph* 2.9 seconds
- *Power* 691 hp

LAMBORGHINI AVENTADOR

The Aventador's angular body is a special lightweight one-piece carbon-fiber shell mounted on aluminum frames. The two distinctive "scissor-action" doors open to reveal a snug two-person cockpit with track-style leather bucket seats and a high-tech digital dashboard controlled by an onboard computer.

A shiny 6.5-liter engine is housed beneath the tailgate.

2013 RANGE ROVER SPORT

James Bond actor Daniel Craig was employed to launch the new Range Rover in a glitzy New York ceremony that ended with him driving through the city in the supercharged V8 version—the fastest Range Rover ever built. The five-liter engine is limited to a 155 mph top speed, but acceleration of the two-ton off-roader is in Porsche territory.

The Sport's aluminum components reduce its weight by up to 925 pounds.

2013 RANGE ROVER SPORT

FEATURES:

- *Engine size* 305 cu. in.
- *Top speed* 155 mph
- *Acceleration 0–60 mph* 4.9 seconds
- *Power* 510 hp

RANGE ROVER SPORT

Its lightweight aluminum makeup makes the Sport fast and fuel-efficient, and gives it sharper, sports-car-like handling. This is also helped by its high-tech adaptive dynamic systems that monitor conditions and driving requirements 500 times per second. And for passengers, there's a huge 1,700-watt stereo with 23 speakers.

The cabin combines high-tech luxury and sportiness.

2013 ROLLS-ROYCE WRAITH

The most powerful Rolls-Royce ever is more like a high-performance, high-technology sports coupé than one of the company's traditional sedate luxury cars. The big Roller may weigh a hefty 5,203 pounds, but the twin-turbo V12 engine with eight-speed automatic gearbox hurries it to a restricted maximum of 155 mph as if it were a lightweight roadster.

The latest Rolls still carries the Spirit of Ecstasy badge.

2013 ROLLS-ROYCE WRAITH

FEATURES:

- *Engine size* 6,592 cu. in.
- *Top speed* 155 mph
- *Acceleration 0–60 mph* 4.4 seconds
- *Power* 624 hp

The enormous doors open from the front.

ROLLS-ROYCE WRAITH

The classically luxurious interior is supplemented by state-of-the-art technology, including a transmission that uses GPS to plan gear changes in advance. A voice-activated "valet service" controls the info-tainment systems, and the cockpit headlining contains 1,340 fiber-optic lamps that simulate a glittering night sky.

Duesenberg Model J

It's no coincidence that this book ends with the fastest Range Rover yet and the most powerful Rolls-Royce ever built.

The demand for high-performance and luxury vehicles like these has driven much of the development of cars over the last 125 years. After all, the very first cars were just a faster, more luxurious alternative to walking or driving a horse and cart.

From the Duesenberg Model J—"the self-proclaimed greatest car in the world"—to today's over-the-top supercar, the Bugatti Veyron, there has always been an engineering imperative to build flashier, fancier, and faster motorcars. And that's probably because

1908 FORD MODEL T

1. Match and stick together tabs 1 through 8 to form the body.
2. Match and stick tabs 9 through 11 to form the front.
3. Use tabs 12 through 16 to stick front to body.
4. Fold wheel-arch and running board pieces into shape.
5. Fold in the small triangles on either side of tab 18, push tab through corresponding slot, fold triangles out again to secure.
6. Stick tab 17 to body and tab 19 to underside of wheel arch.
7. Repeat the process for tabs 20 through 22.
8. Stick tabs 23 and 24 to back of wheels.

1910 CADILLAC MODEL 30

1. Match and stick together tabs 1 through 8 to form the body.
2. Stick tabs 9 and 10 to midsection windshield piece.
3. Match and stick tabs 11 through 14 to shape the front.
4. Fold in the small triangles on either side of tabs 15 and 16, push tabs through corresponding slots, fold triangles out again to secure. Stick tabs 17 and 18 to running boards.
5. Fold in 19 and 20, push tabs through corresponding slots, fold tabs out again to secure.
6. Fold in the small triangles on either side of 21 and 22, push tabs through corresponding slots, fold triangles out again. Stick tab 23 to running board. Repeat the process for tabs 24 through 26.
7. Stick tabs 19 and 20, 27 and 28 to wheels.
8. Stick tab 29 to running board and tab 30 to the body.

1928 DUESENBERG MODEL J

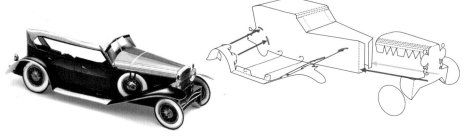

1. Match and stick together tabs 1 through 8 to form the body.
2. Fold and form the front piece. Match and stick tabs 9 through 14 to the body.
3. Match and stick 15 and 16 onto the front.
4. Fold in the small triangles on either side of tabs 17 through 20, push tabs through corresponding slots, fold triangles out again to secure. Stick 21 through 25 to the body.
5. Repeat the process for tabs 26 through 33.
6. Stick tabs 34 and 35 to the wheels.

1929 BENTLEY BLOWER

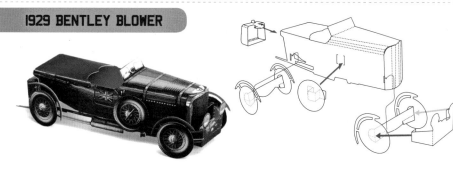

1. Match and stick together tabs 1 through 4 to form the body.
2. Match and stick tabs 5 through 8 to form the rear piece.
3. Fold in the small triangles on either side of tab 9, push tab through corresponding slot, fold triangles out again to secure.
5. Stick tab 10 to bottom of rear piece.
6. Fold in 11a and 12a, push tabs through corresponding slots, fold 11a and 12a out again to secure.
7. Repeat the process for 13a and 14a.
8. Stick 15 and 16 to front axle.
9. Push 17 and 18 through corresponding slots and stick down.
10. Stick 11, 12, 13, 14, and 19 to the wheels.

someone, somewhere, is always prepared to pay extra for a bigger, bolder, and better-equipped car.

So will cars continue to get faster and faster? Will there always be huge, gas-guzzling vehicles like the Hummer? Will we continue to build sports cars that go a lot faster than any speed limit in the world, such as the Lamborghini Aventador? Is there a future for all-wheel-drive rally

Hummer H3

1930 PACKARD EIGHT

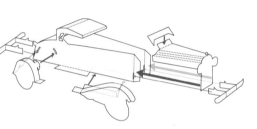

1. Match and stick together tabs 1 through 10 to form the body.
2. Stick tabs 11 and 12 to the body, and 13 and 14 to the front.
3. Stick the two small tabs to shape the front; stick to the body at 13 and 14.
4. Stick tab 15 to windshield.
5. Stick 16 through 19 to form front wheel arch; stick 20 to the body and 21 to the running board. Repeat for 22 through 27.
6. Stick tabs 28 and 29 to form rear wheel arch. Fold in the small triangles on either side of tabs 30 and 31, push through corresponding slots, fold triangles out again to secure. Stick 32 to running board. Repeat the process for 33 through 37.
7. Stick 38 and then insert 39 and 40 into front slots on the body.
8. Repeat the process for 41 through 43.

1932 FORD MODEL B

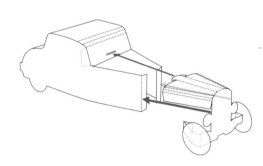

1. Match and stick together tabs 1 through 10 to form the body.
2. Fold in the small triangles on either side of tab 11, push tab through corresponding slot, fold triangles out again to secure.
3. Stick 12 and 13 to the body. Fold around to form front piece. Match and stick 14 and 15.
4. Stick 16 and 17 to the body.
5. Stick 18 and 19 to the wheels.

1933 AUTO UNION TYPE C

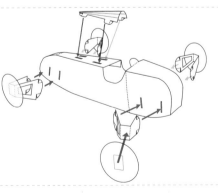

1. Match and stick together tabs 1 through 12 to form the body.
2. Fold in the small triangles on either side of tabs 13 and 14, push tabs through corresponding slots, fold triangles out again to secure.
3. Repeat process for 15 and 16, 17 and 18, 19 and 20.
4. Fold in the small triangles at the side of tabs 21 through 24, push tabs through corresponding slots, fold triangles out again to secure.
5. Stick the wheels to 26 through 29.

1934 CHRYSLER AIRFLOW

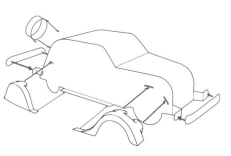

1. Match and stick together tabs 1 through 8 to form the body.
2. Stick tabs 9 and 10 to form front wheel arch.
3. Fold in the small triangles on either side of tabs 11 and 12, push tabs through corresponding slots, fold triangles out again. Stick tab 13 to running board. Repeat process for 14 through 18.
4. Match and stick tabs 19 through 21 to form rear wheel arch.
5. Fold in the small triangles on either side of tabs 22 and 23, push through corresponding slots, fold triangles out again to secure. Stick tab 24 to running board. Repeat process for 25 through 30.
6. Stick 31 and 32, 33 and 34 to front and rear bumpers.
7. Stick 35 to form spare wheel; insert 36 and 37 into corresponding slots.

cars for the road, such as the Subaru Impreza? Having looked at a selection of the most interesting and memorable cars of the last hundred years for this book, can we guess what the cars of the future will be like?

Well, we all know that motorized transport has been on a collision course with the environment for decades. Around the world, this has resulted in increasing legal controls on exhaust emissions and pressure on carmakers to explore more environmentally friendly technologies.

Some of the later cars in this book hint at new "green" directions for the motor industry.

Slowly but surely, huge multinational carmakers are adjusting their sights to take into account the environmental impact of what they produce. Look at the Mercedes SLS AMG, for example.

Lamborghini Aventador

1937 BUGATTI TYPE 57 ATLANTIC

1. Match and stick together tabs 1 through 11 to form the body, insert and stick 12 into corresponding slot.
2. Match and stick 13 and 14, insert 15 into corresponding slot.
3. Match and stick 16 through 21 to form front wheel arches.
4. Fold in the small triangles on either side of tabs 22 and 23, push tabs through corresponding slots, fold triangles out to secure. Stick tab 24. Repeat process for 25 through 27.
5. Fold in the small triangles on either side of tabs 28 and 29, push tabs through corresponding slots, fold triangles out again to secure. Stick tab 30 to body.
6. Fold in the small triangles on either side of tabs 31 and 32, push tabs through corresponding slots, fold triangles out again to secure.

1939 VOLKSWAGEN BEETLE

1. Match and stick together tabs 1 through 12 to form the body.
2. Match and stick tabs 13 through 16 to form rear wheel arches.
3. Fold in the small triangles on either side of tabs 17 and 18, push tabs through corresponding slots, fold triangles out again to secure. Stick tabs 19 and 20 to the running boards.
4. Match and stick tabs 21 through 24 to form front wheel arches.
5. Fold in the small triangles on either side of tabs 25 and 26, push tabs through corresponding slots, fold triangles out again to secure. Stick tabs 27 and 28 to the running boards.

1941 WILLYS JEEP

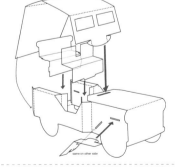

1. Match and stick together tab 1, insert tabs 2 and 3 into corresponding slots to form the body.
2. Match and stick tabs 4 through 6 to roof piece.
3. Match and stick 7 and 8 to front seats. Insert tab into corresponding slot.
4. Insert tabs 10 through 13 into corresponding slots to form the back seats. Stick 14 to back of roof piece.
5. Fold in the small triangles on either side of tab 15, push through corresponding slot, fold triangles out again to secure.
6. Insert tabs 16 through 19 into corresponding slots to form front wheel arches.
7. Fold radiator down, match and stick 20 and 21.

1948 CITROEN 2CV

1. Match and stick together tabs 1 through 16 to form the body.
2. Fold in the small triangles on either side of tabs 17 through 19, push tabs through corresponding slots, fold triangles out again to secure.
3. Repeat process for tabs 20 through 22.

Mercedes-Benz was there at the very start of the history of cars. It's still there and still expanding the technical boundaries. Yes, the SLS is an exciting supercar—but did you notice that it's also available as an all-electric version that uses a pioneering system of one emission-free motor per wheel? This SLS AMG Coupé Electric Drive is perhaps the world's first eco-supercar.

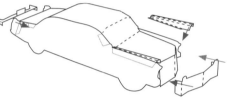

Mercedes SLS AMG
Coupé Electric Drive

1954 CADILLAC FLEETWOOD 60

1. Match and stick together tabs 1 through 10 to form the body.
2. Match and stick tabs 11 through 13 to form the front.
3. Match and stick together tabs 14 through 17 to form the front wings.
4. Match and stick tabs 18 and 19 to complete the front.
5. Match and stick tabs 20 and 21 to attach the rear bumper.

1955 CITROEN DS

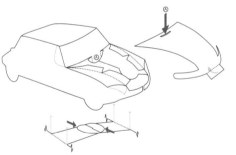

1. Match and stick together tabs 1 through 14 to form the body.
2. Slot together and stick 15 and 16.
3. Fold in the small triangles on either side of tab 17, push tab through corresponding slot, fold triangles out again to secure.
4. Match and stick together 18 through 21 to form front.
5. Stick 22 and 23 to bumper.
6. Fold over and stick 24 to reverse of bumper.

1956 CHECKER MOTOR CORPORATION A8

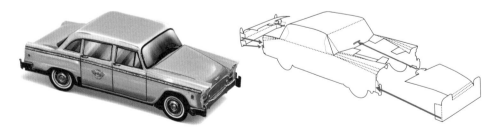

1. Match and stick together tabs 1 through 4 to form the body.
2. Fold in the small triangles on either side of tab 5, push tab through corresponding slot, fold triangles out again to secure.
3. Match and stick together tabs 6 through 11 to form front piece.
4. Fold in the small triangles on either side of tab 12, push tab through corresponding slot, fold triangles out again to secure.
5. Match and stick together tabs 13 through 20 to form back piece.

1957 VEB TRABANT

1. Match and stick together tabs 1 through 4 to form the body.
2. Fold in the small triangles on either side of tab 5, push tab through corresponding slot, fold triangles out again to secure.
3. Match and stick together tabs 6 through 11 to form front piece.
4. Match and stick together tabs 12 through 18 to form back piece.

And what about the exotic 250-mph Koenigsegg CCX? Some versions of this super sports coupé have become the world's most expensive cars. But at the same time, the specialist Swedish carmaker offers its wealthy buyers an extraordinary optional extra: a sophisticated adaptation that allows the CCX to run on an environmentally friendly fuel that can be made from potatoes.

Koenigsegg CCX

1959 ALFA ROMEO GIULIETTA SPIDER

1. Match and stick together tabs 1 and 2 to form the rear.
2. Match and stick together 3 through 7 to form front.
3. Fold over radiator and stick tabs 8 and 9.
4. Bend windshield into position.

1959 AUSTIN MINI

1. Match and stick together tabs 1 through 6 to form the body.
2. Fold around front of car, match and stick tabs 7 through 12.
3. Attach front bumper section to front.

1961 JAGUAR E-TYPE SERIES I

1. Match and stick together tabs 1 through 10 to form the body.
2. Match and stick tabs 11 through 14 to complete the rear.
3. Stick 15 through 18 to form front wings and headlights.
4. Stick 19 through 24 to form hood and complete wings.
5. Fold down front of car and stick tabs 27 through 30, tuck in tabs 25 and 26 behind headlight/radiator area.

1962 FERRARI 250 GTO

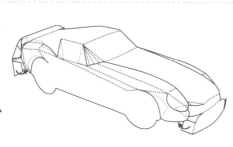

1. Match and stick together tabs 1 through 6 to form the body.
2. Form spoiler and stick tabs 7 and 8.
3. Match and stick tabs 9 through 12 to complete rear.
4. Stick 13 through 16 to form front wings and headlights.
5. Stick 17 through 22 to form hood and complete wings.
6. Fold down front of car and stick tabs 25 through 28, tuck in tabs 23 and 24 behind headlight/radiator area.

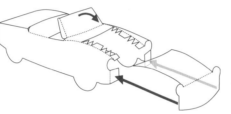

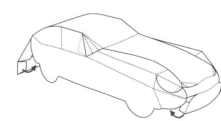

The humble Toyota Prius is the car that perhaps points to the most achievable future for automobiles. Using hybrid technology, this unassuming Japanese hatchback has become a symbol of environmentally friendly driving. With a list of customers that includes many Hollywood superstars, perhaps it's no surprise that more and more manufacturers have launched hybrid versions of their own cars in the last decade.

So from an environmental point of view, there is hope of compromise. Beautiful, luxurious, fast cars that have minimal environmental impact can indeed be created. Much progress has already been made. Developments such as catalytic converters, more efficient engines,

Toyota Prius

108

1963 ASTON MARTIN DB5

1. Match and stick together tabs 1 through 8 to form the body.
2. Match and stick tabs 9 through 14 to form the hood.
3. Stick tabs 15 and 16 to body, tucking 17 and 18 behind headlights.
4. Fold down the headlights and stick to tabs 19 and 20.
5. Match and stick 21 through 28 to complete the rear.

1963 PORCHE 911

1. Fold in the small triangles on either side of tab 1, push tab through corresponding slot, fold triangles out again to secure.
2. Match and stick together tabs 2 through 7 to form the roof and windshield.
3. Fold in the small triangles on either side of tabs 8 and 9, push tabs through corresponding slots, fold triangles out again to secure.
4. Match and stick tabs 10 through 15 to form the hood. Stick 16 and 17 to the back of the headlights. Tuck 20 and 21 behind tabs 18 and 19. Stick 18 and 19 to the bumper.
5. Match and stick tabs 22 through 27 to form the rear.

1963 AC CARS SHELBY COBRA

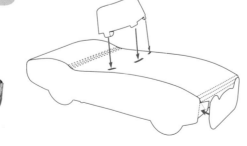

1. Match and stick together tabs 1 through 14 to form the body.
2. Stick tabs 15 through 18 to complete the rear.
3. Fold headlight/radiator piece around and stick 19 and 20 to complete the front.
4. Fold in the small triangles at the side of tabs 21 and 22, push tabs through corresponding slots, fold triangles out again to secure.

1964 FORD GT40

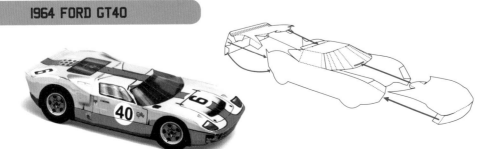

1. Match and stick together tabs 1 and 2 to form the windshield.
2. Fold in the small triangles on either side of tab 3, push tab through corresponding slot, fold triangles out again to secure.
3. Match and stick tabs 4 through 9 to form front piece.
4. Fold in the small triangles on either side of tab 10, push tab through corresponding slot, fold triangles out again to secure.
5. Match and stick tabs 11 through 18 to form rear piece.
6. Stick 19 and 20 to complete the rear.

and the introduction of unleaded fuel have helped dramatically cut the pollution caused by internal combustion engines. Even the most mainstream cars are now more fuel-efficient and greener than ever before. More of the cars themselves can be recycled, too.

Behind the scenes, manufacturers' research departments are working in many different directions to find the type of vehicle that we will be driving through the rest of the century. Different engineers and scientists champion different possibilities. Will future cars run on biodiesel, hydrogen fuel cells, electricity, or ethanol? Will some extraordinary new propulsion system be invented that we can't even guess at yet?

Or will the cars of the future actually be a more gradual evolution of present hybrid technologies using sophisticated combinations of electric and gas engines to keep emissions to an absolute minimum? That's the solution many car experts suspect is most likely.

BMW i3

109

1964 FORD MUSTANG MARK I

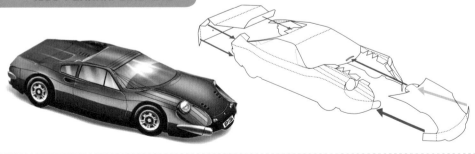

1. Match and stick together tabs 1 through 12 to form the body.
2. Stick 13 and 14 to the back of the headlights.
3. Fold down radiator grille and stick 15 and 16.
4. Match and stick 17 through 20 to complete the front.

1967 CHEVROLET CORVETTE STINGRAY

1. Fold in the small triangles on either side of tabs 1 and 2, push tabs through corresponding slots, fold triangles out again to secure. Stick tab 3 to form the front.
2. Match and stick together tabs 4 through 13 to form the body.
3. Stick tabs 14 through 18 to form the roof and windshield piece.
4. Fold in the small triangles at the side of tabs 19 and 20, push tabs through corresponding slots, fold triangles out again to secure.
5. Stick tabs 21 and 22 into corresponding slots on the side of the body. Insert tab 23 into corresponding slot on hood.

1969 FERRARI DINO 246

1. Match and stick together tabs 1 through 8 to form the body.
2. Fold rear piece into shape, then match and stick together tabs 9 through 17 to complete the rear.
3. Fold in the small triangles on either side of tab 18, push tab through corresponding slot, fold triangles out again to secure.
4. Match and stick 19 through 22 to form the hood.
5. Fold over front of hood and stick 23 and 24.
6. Stick tabs 25 and 26 to the underside of the hood to form the curved headlight bays.
7. Fold down headlights.

1969 PONTIAC GTO

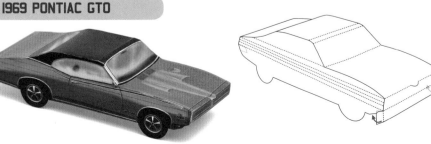

1. Match and stick together tabs 1 through 14 to form the body.
2. Fold down the radiator grille and stick tabs 15 and 16 to complete the front.
3. Match and stick tabs 17 through 20 to complete the rear.

The iconic and innovative cars in this book, such as the VW Beetle and Austin Mini, show that great technical advances can come from unexpected sources, and that we may be surprised by something that's just around the corner.

If you've built all 50 of the car models in the previous pages by now, you'll have a pretty good understanding of how car bodies have evolved since the Model T's box-on-wheels design. The body shapes of cars such as the Dodge Viper or DeLorean demonstrate this move toward aircraft-influenced aerodynamic designs. Auto engineers have increasingly realized that aerodynamics can influence speed and efficiency just as much as engine size and power. Since the Chrysler Airflow of 1934, cars have become sleeker over the decades.

VW Beetle

1974 LAMBORGHINI COUNTACH

1. Match and stick together tabs 1 through 8 to form the body.
2. Stick tabs 9 through 12 to form the hood.
3. Fold front down and stick tabs 13 and 14.
4. Fold under and stick tabs 15 and 16.
5. Fold rear piece into shape, stick tabs 17 through 19.
6. Fold down and stick tabs 20 through 23.
7. Complete rear by folding under and sticking tabs 24 and 25 through body interior.
8. Stick tabs 26 and 27 to form right-hand headlight.
9. Fold in the small triangles on either side of tab 28, push tab through corresponding slot, fold triangles out again to secure. Insert tab 29 into corresponding slot on hood.
10. Repeat process for tabs 30 through 33.

1976 GM HOLDEN UTE HX

1. Match and stick together tabs 1 through 10 to form the body.
2. Fold down front and stick tabs 11 through 14.
3. Match and stick tabs 15 through 18 to form tailgate.

1977 PONTIAC FIREBIRD TRANS AM

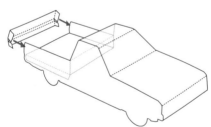

1. Match and stick together tabs 1 through 6 to form the body.
2. Fold spoiler into shape and stick tabs 7 and 8.
3. Match and stick tabs 9 through 12 to complete the rear.
4. Stick tabs 13 through 16 to form hood.
5. Bend front piece into shape and stick tabs 17 through 19.
6. Stick tabs 20 through 22.
7. Fold under and stick tabs 23 and 24 to interior of the body.

1980 AUDI QUATTRO

1. Match and stick together tabs 1 through 10 to form the body.
2. Fold front into shape, stick tabs 11 through 14.
3. Fold under and stick tabs 15 and 16 to interior of body.
4. Fold down rear and stick tabs 17 through 22.
5. Fold spoiler into shape. Fold in the small triangles on either side of tabs 23 and 24, push tabs through corresponding slots, fold triangles out again to secure.
6. Fold and match 25 and 26 on the back of the headlights.
7. Stick headlights to front bumper.

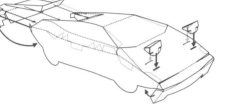

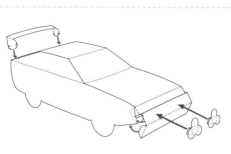

Modern supercars such as the McLaren F1 and Honda NSX have taken the aerodynamic lessons of Formula 1 and transferred them to the road. Expect this trend to continue. Cars will surely continue to get lower to the ground and more aerodynamic to slip through the air with less resistance.

Along with this, the materials used are getting lighter. The Ford GT40 used this formula to great effect—putting a big, powerful engine in a lightweight fiberglass body enables sensational performance. Modern cars increasingly use materials such as plastic, glass fiber, carbon, Kevlar, and aluminum to reduce weight. Expect more cars to swap heavy steel panels for materials like these.

The popularity of off-road SUVs following the pioneering Willys Jeep showed that one type of car didn't suit everyone. Some wanted a small family car like the Citroën 2CV, others wanted a pickup truck like the Holden Ute. The Smart FourTwo

Aerodynamic Formula 1 design

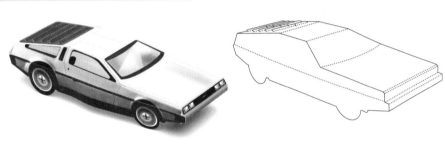

111

1981 DELOREAN DMC

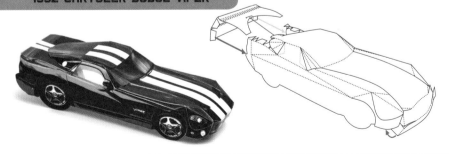

1. Match and stick together tabs 1 through 6 to form the body.
2. Fold front section into shape, then stick tabs 7 through 10.
3. Fold rear section into shape, then stick tabs 11 through 14.
4. Fold up rear window spoilers.

1990 HONDA NSX

1. Match and stick together tabs 1 through 8 to form the body.
2. Fold front piece into shape. Stick tabs 9 and 10.
3. Match and stick tabs 11 through 16 to join front piece to body.
4. Fold back piece into shape.
5. Match and stick tabs 17 through 22 to join back piece to body.
6. Fold spoiler into shape.
7. Fold in the small triangles at the side of tabs 23 through 26, push tabs through corresponding slots, fold triangles out again to secure.

1992 CHRYSLER DODGE VIPER

1. Match and stick together tabs 1 through 4 to form the windshield and roof piece.
2. Stick tabs 5 and 6 to form the front of the wing.
3. Repeat for 7 and 8.
4. Stick tabs 9 through 14 to form the hood.
5. Fold back piece into shape.
6. Fold in the small triangles on either side of tab 15, push tab through corresponding slot, fold triangles out again to secure.
7. Match and stick tabs 16 through 25 to complete rear.
8. Fold front into shape, tuck in 28 through 31, and stick tabs 26 and 27 to the interior of the body.

1992 MCLAREN F1

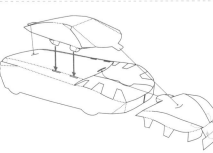

1. Fold in the small triangles on either side of tab 1, push tab through corresponding slot, fold triangles out again to secure.
2. Stick tabs 2 and 3 to form the hood.
3. Match and stick 4 through 15 to join the hood to the body. Fold over and stick 16 to complete front.
4. Stick 17 through 22 to form the rear.
5. Match and stick tabs 23 through 26 to form the roof section.
6. Fold in the small triangles at the side of tabs 27 through 30, push tabs through corresponding slots, fold triangles out again to secure.
7. Insert tabs 31 and 32 into their corresponding slots.

is big enough for some buyers, while others feel they need to be driven around in a bulletproof Cadillac.

We suspect this trend toward niche vehicles will continue. Expect more sporty crossovers, mini SUVs, luxury hatchbacks, four-wheel-drive sports cars, and load-carrying family cars to appear—and probably plenty of categories we haven't even thought of yet.

Cars such as the Alfa Romeo Giulietta Spider in the 1950s or the E-Type Jaguar in the 1960s suggest that there will always be some that are memorable purely because they look so good and so right for their time. And they don't necessarily have to be supercars: the Audi TT and Ford Mustang were real head-turners, and yet affordable to most customers at the time.

Alfa Romeo Giulietta Spider

1992 GENERAL MOTORS HUMMER HI

1. Match and stick together tabs 1 through 6 to form the front of the body.
2. Match and stick together tabs 7 through 12 to form the rear of the body.
3. Fold spare wheel into shape and stick tab 13.
4. Insert tabs 14 and 15 into corresponding slots.

1997 TOYOTA PRIUS

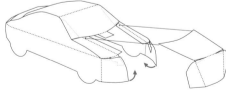

1. Match and stick together tabs 1 through 6 to form the front of the body.
2. Match and stick together tabs 7 through 12 to form the rear of the body.
3. Shape front piece and stick tab 13 to the left and 14 to the right. Stick tab 15 to the back of this piece to complete the front.

1998 AUDI TT

1. Match and stick together tabs 1 through 10 to form the body.
2. Fold front piece into shape. Match and stick tabs 11 through 15 to join front piece to the body.
3. Match and stick tabs 16 through 23 to form the rear.

1999 BMW Z8

1. Match and stick together tabs 1 through 4 to shape the back and front wings.
2. Match and stick tabs 5 through 12 to form the body.
3. Fold down and stick tabs 13 and 14 to complete the rear.
4. Fold front piece into shape. Stick tabs 15 through 20 to form the hood.
5. Stick tabs 21 and 22 to complete the front.

We can't predict the future, but some things are certain. Drivers around the world will continue to enjoy whatever type of motoring is available to them. Even if we were all forced to drive around in exactly the same car, doubtless someone in a shed somewhere would be trying to make his or hers go a bit faster than everyone else's.

The car of the future is likely to be more aerodynamic, lighter, more fuel-efficient, less polluting, and safer—but still lots of fun to drive. We hope that in 100 years' time there will still be books about cars, just like this one, and readers like you to enjoy reading about them.

The shape of things to come?

2005 SUBARU IMPREZA

1. Match and stick together tabs 1 through 8 to form the body.
2. Match and stick tabs 9 through 12 to form the rear.
3. Fold rear bumper into shape. Fold in the small triangles on either side of tabs 13 and 14, push tabs through corresponding slots, fold triangles out again to secure.
4. Fold in the small triangles on either side of tabs 15 and 16, push tabs through corresponding slots, fold triangles out again to secure.
5. Match and stick tabs 17 through 22 to complete the front.
6. Fold spoiler into shape, stick together at 23, and stick to rear at 24.

2005 BUGATTI VEYRON

1. Match and stick together tabs 1 through 5 to form the front and rear wings. Repeat process for tabs 6 through 10.
2. Match and stick 11 through 17 to complete the rear.
3. Stick 18 through 21 to form the windshield.
4. Stick 22 and bend front piece into shape.
5. Match and stick 23 through 26 to join the hood to the body, insert tab 25 into corresponding slot on the windshield.

2006 KOENIGSEGG CCX

1. Match and stick together tabs 1 through 6 to form the front wings.
2. Stick 7 and 8 to form the shape of the roof and windshield.
3. Stick 9 through 14 to join roof to body.
4. Stick 15 and 16 to form rear wings.
5. Fold rear piece into shape. Stick 17 through 23 to complete rear.
6. Fold in the small triangles on either side of tab 24, push tab through corresponding slot, fold triangles out to secure.
7. Stick tabs 25 through 30 to join hood to body.
8. Fold down front of hood and tuck behind headlights.
9. Stick 31 and 32 to back of headlights.

2007 AUDI R8

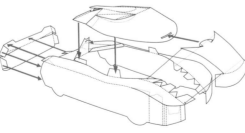

1. Match and stick together tabs 1 through 10 to form the body.
2. Fold hood and radiator piece into shape. Match and stick tabs 11 through 16.
3. Stick tabs 17 through 20 to back of headlights.
4. Stick tabs 21 through 24 to the interior of the wheel arches.

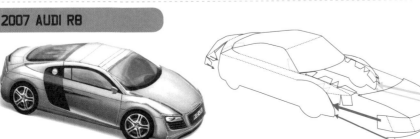

114

2008 DAIMLER SMART FORTWO

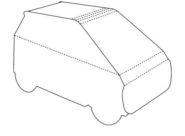

1. Match and stick together tabs 1 through 6 to form the front of the vehicle.
2. Match and stick together tabs 7 through 10 to form the rear of the vehicle.

2009 CADILLAC ONE

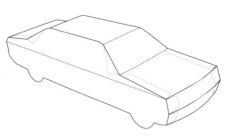

1. Match and stick together tabs 1 through 8 to form the front of the vehicle.
2. Match and stick together tabs 9 through 14 to form the rear of the vehicle.

2010 MERCEDES SLS AMG

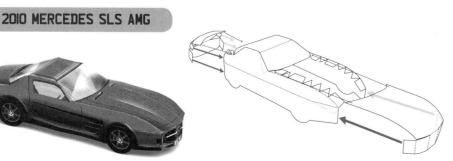

1. Match and stick together tabs 1 through 8 to form the body.
2. Fold front piece into shape, then stick tabs 9 through 14. Fold down front piece and stick tabs 15 and 16 to the interior of the wings.
3. Fold rear piece into shape, then stick tabs 17 through 20.
4. Fold down and stick 21 through 24 to complete the rear.

2011 LAMBORGHINI AVENTADOR

1. Match and stick together tabs 1 through 6 to form the body.
2. Fold door vents into shape, stick tabs 7 through 9. Then stick 10 through 12. Repeat process for tabs 13 through 18.
3. Stick tabs 19 through 24 to form roof section.
4. Stick roof piece to body using tabs 25 through 34.
5. Fold rear piece into shape, then stick tabs 35 through 40.
6. Fold front radiator grille piece into shape, then stick tabs 41 through 44.

2013 RANGE ROVER SPORT

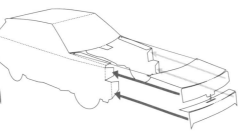

1. Match and stick together tabs 1 through 10 to form the body.
2. Match and stick hood piece using tabs 11 through 15.
3. Stick the final front piece into position using tabs 16 and 17.
4. Insert tab 18 into corresponding slot.

2013 ROLLS-ROYCE WRAITH

1. Match and stick together tabs 1 through 6 to form the windshield and hood.
2. Match and stick tabs 7 through 14 to form the rear.
3. Fold front into shape, tuck 17 and 18 behind tabs 15 and 16. Stick 15 and 16 to back of headlights.
4. Stick 19 and 20 to complete front.

PICTURE CREDITS

Key: m = middle, t = top, l = left r, = right

Photographs
AKG IMAGES: p7 mr / p23 t ALAMY: Everett Collection Historical p1 t / Universal Images Group p1 tr / Pep Roig p6 mr / p8 tr / imagebroker p9 t / Goddard Automotive p11 t, p35 t / BlueMoon Stock p12 tr / Motoring Picture Library p14 mr, p39 t, p40 tr / TONY WILSON-BLIGH p15 t / Edward Herdwick 18 tr / Performance Images p21 t / Phil Talbot p22 t, p45 t, p60 tr / culture-images GmbH p25 t, p41 t, p86 tr, p89 ts / Rolf Adlercreutz p27 t / Pictorial Press Ltd p27 mr, p64 tr, p68 tr / Matthew Richardson p28 tr, p47 t / simon clay 30 t / pbpgalleries p37 t / Lordprice Collection p38 t / nawson p43 t / Photos 12 p43 mr / picturesbyrob p46 tr, p100 tr / Stuart Hickling p49 t / AF archive p52 t / p53 t / p58 t / Jason Knott p61 t / Richard McDowell p62 t / ilian car p63 t / Action Plus Sports Images p65 t / Stephen Barnes/Transport p67 t / p71 t / p73 t / Maurice Savage p79 t / p79 t / Drive Images p80 t / Chris Willson p81 t / Adrian Sherratt p84 t / Dudarev Mikhail p87 t (background) / Mark Dyball p91 t / Urbanmyth p92 tr / Lisa Werner p102 t CORBIS: p5 t / Martyn Goddard p19 t / Car Culture p20 t, p42 t / Betmann p32 tr / SHAWN THEW/epa p93 t / Brooks Kraft p94 tr / Transtock p97 t H. Lorren Au Jr/Zuma Press p98 tr / Car Culture p105 / Blair Bunting/Transtock p107 t / TIM WIMBORNE/Reuters p108 t / Horacio Villalobos p109 t MARY EVANS: Epic/Tallandier p29 t (background) GETTY IMAGES: Three Lions p3 t / Car Culture p4 mr, p7 t / p9 t (background) / p13 t (background) / p33 t / SIM p51 t / Rainer W. Schlegelmilch p55 t / Popular Science p69 t / p83 t / p88 t / p92 mr / Bloomberg p99 t / p101 t MOMD: by kind permission p56 r SHUTTERSTOCK: nadi555 p5 t / justasc p17 t / MarekPiotrowski p19 t (background) / littleny p21 t (background), p31 t (background) / somchaij p27 t (background) / Jule_Berlin p34 t / Radoslow Lecyk p36 t / godrick p39 t (background) / Digital Media Pro p48 t / Ditty_abot_summer p55 t (background) / Raffaella Calzoni p57 t (background) / C.J.Williamson p59 t (background) /Ralph Loesche p61 t (background) / prochasson frederic p63 t (background) / vvoe p67 t (background) / Brad Remy p72 t / Carlos Caetano p73 t (background) / Philip Lange p75 t / AHMAD FAIZAL YAHYA p77 t / GuoZhongHua p78 tr / Max Earey p85 t, p95 t / Olga Besnard p96 t / BassKwong p97 t (background) / djgis p99 t (background) / zhangyang13576997233 p103 t / Michael Shake p104 t / Fingerhut p106 t / f9photos p110 t / Nuno Andre p111 t / Visaro p113 t WIKIPEDIA: Ben Sutherland p10 t / Sicnag p13 t, p54 t, p57 t / L. Kenzel p16 t / Randy Stern p17 t / US National Archive p23 mr, p24 tr / Lebubu93 p26 mr / Joe Mabel p29 t / Jim.henderson p31 t / Herranderssvensson p44 tr / Mr.choppers p50 tr / Brian Snelson p59 t / Ypy31 p70 tr / Sfoskett p74 t / Affemitwaffe p82 t / Trubble p87 t / James086 p90 tr

Illustrations
STEFANO AZZALIN: p13 b / p14 ml / p14 b / p33 b / p34 ml / p34 b / p51 b / p52 m / p52 b / p57 b / p58 m / p73 b / p74 ml / p74 b / p85 b / p86 m / p86 m NIGEL CHILVERS: p23 b / p24 ml / p26 b / p29 b / p30 ml / p30 b / p35 b / p36 ml / p36 b / p39 b / p40 m / p40 b / p43 b / p44 m / p44 b / p45 b / p46 m / p46 b / p53 b / p54 m / p54 b / p55 b / p56 m / p56 b / p59 b / p60 m / p60 b / p61 b / p62 ml / p62 b / p67 b / p68 ml / p68 b / p69 b / p70 ml / p70 b / p77 b / p78 ml / p78 b / p80 ml / p80 b / p81 b / p82 m / p82 b / p83 b / p84 ml / p84 b / p87 b / p88 m / p88 b / p89 b / p90 m / p90 b / p91 b / p92 ml / p92 b / p93 b / p94 b / p94 b / p95 / p96 m / p96 b / p97 b / p98 m / p98 b / p99 b / p100 ml / p100 b / p101 b / p102 m / p102 b ANDREW CROWSON: p27 b / p28 m / p28 b / p79 b/ p112 t MAT EDWARDS: p5 b / p6 ml / p6 b / p9 b / p10 ml / p10 b / p11 b / p12 ml / p12 b / p15 b / p16 ml / p16 b / p21 b / p22 ml / p22 b / p25 b / p26 ml / p26 b / p37 b / p38 m / p38 b / p41 b / p42 ml / p42 b / p47 b / p48 m / p48 b / p63 b / p64 m / p64 b JERRY PYKE: p7 b / p8 ml / p8 b / p17 b / p18 ml / p18 b / p19 b / p20 ml / p20 b / p31 b / p32 ml / p32 b / p49 b / p50 m / p50 b / p65 b / p66 m / p66 b / p71 b / p72 ml / p72 b / p75 b / p76 ml / p76 b

116